THE
LIBERAL ARTS
ADVANTAGE

THE LIBERAL ARTS ADVANTAGE

How to Turn Your Degree Into a Great Job

GREGORY GIANGRANDE

AVON BOOKS ◆ NEW YORK

AVON BOOKS, INC.
1350 Avenue of the Americas
New York, New York 10019

Copyright © 1998 by Gregory Giangrande
Interior design by Rhea Braunstein
Published by arrangement with the author
Visit our website at **http://www.AvonBooks.com**
ISBN: 0-380-79567-1

Library of Congress Cataloging in Publication Data:

Giangrande, Gregory.
   The liberal arts advantage : how to turn your degree into a great job /
Gregory Giangrande.
       p. cm.
   1. Job hunting.   2. Vocational guidance.   I. Title.
HF5382.7.G53   1998   97-49053
650.14—dc21   CIP

First Avon Books Trade Printing: June 1998

AVON TRADEMARK REG. U.S. PAT. OFF. AND IN OTHER COUNTRIES, MARCA
REGISTRADA, HECHO EN U.S.A.

Printed in the U.S.A.

OPM   10 9 8 7 6 5 4 3 2 1

For Elias Atticus Giangrande—my son

Everything should be made as simple as possible . . .
but not simpler.

Albert Einstein

Contents

Acknowledgments

There are many people who directly and indirectly have contributed to this book, and my ability to be in the position to write it.

My wife, my love, Sheila Giangrande—whose warmth feeds our son Elias's soul daily, as she selflessly puts her own career ambitions on hold. Who graciously changed more than her share of diapers, and labored over more than her share of chores, so that I could have time to write. Thank you for your support, love, encouragement, and patience—especially when you said my all-nighters and all-work-and-no-play were turning me into Jack Nicholson. If we are lucky, Elias's friends will be using the 11th edition of this book when he graduates from college 18 years from now, and we won't have to worry about how to pay for college.

My grandfather, John Mandato, an inspiration who still goes into the office at the age of 86. Thanks for praying every night that I would meet my deadline. Next time though, please start praying a little earlier so that I don't cut it so close. My dad, Joseph Giangrande, one of the few true winners out in Las Vegas, who taught me that if you play the percentages, you'll always be a winner.

Tia Maggini my editor, whose sharp eye kept me focused, and deft touch trimmed (okay sometimes carved) the fat in all the right places. Thank you for the idea, for your steady guidance, and especially your patience as I milked every minute out of every deadline and extension. Lou Aronica, Mike Greenstein and Bill Wright, thank you for saying yes. Tom Dupree, thanks for the great title. A heart felt thank you to everyone else at Avon Books and the entire Hearst Book Group whose hands in some way touched this project.

Thanks to all of the students I've taught and applicants I've met over the years who provided me with so much material. I want to thank my students from the spring of 1997 Speech Class for their research: Claudine Sarraf, Katherine Guintu, Jonathan Ziegel, Kelly Wilsey, Elizabeth Cunningham, Becky Ettlinger, Brad Crater, JuAnne Ng, Nausheen Hussain, Avani Vashi, Joumana Ramji, Utavie Iniya, Steven Rosefort, Mihir Shah, Jaime Meehan, Sunny Tam, Andrew Chan, Avi Jagwani, Sachin Jhangiani, Tsion Bensusan, Mary Rodas, Ralph Gabay, Lindsay Salz, Joia Goldfein and Tommy Mei.

Patty Flatz, thanks for the start in human resources. Christine Names, thanks for opening doors. Debbie Borisoff, thanks for my teaching career. Stephen Foreht—my friend who had nothing to do with this book or my career—but who will get a kick out of being mentioned.

And finally, my mom—Judith Giangrande. Did you think I'd forget you? Thank you for your unwavering love, encouragement and support throughout my entire life. Even though I had to do things my way, I was always listening. I think I get it now. Thank you for cooking the best Italian food in the world. with all the love in the world.

Introduction

Have you heard this one yet?

The graduate with a science degree asks, "Why does it work?"
The graduate with an engineering degree asks, "How does it work?"
The graduate with an accounting degree asks, "How much will it cost?"
The graduate with a liberal arts degree asks, "Do you want fries with that?"

You must admit, that one is funny. Much more original than the same old, "What are you going to do with *that* degree?" Or "You're an English major?" (substitute history, philosophy, sociology, etc.) "Which grade level will you be teaching?"

Like most liberal arts majors, you probably sailed through college smoothly and confidently, pursing your studies the first few years, happily avoiding the issues of job and career. Then, senior year, second semester hit, and the panic set in. Suddenly, the question you've been asked rhetorically for three years seems like a national interrogation: "What *are* you going to do with that degree?"

You become acutely aware that everyone else seems to have had jobs or interviews lined up for months; yet you haven't even stepped foot inside the career development office. I know exactly how you are feeling. You, like many liberal arts majors, have questions and concerns about finding a job. "Perhaps they were right," you think, "maybe I should have majored in something more practical." I'm here to tell you that you are more prepared for the job market than you realize.

The genesis of such stereotypical perspectives on liberal arts studies can be partially attributed to the technological and industrial revolutions that have dominated our country's short history. These revolutions increased the demand for workers with specialized skills, providing them with clearer and more direct links to employment.

So, are you disadvantaged by your course of study? Not at all. In fact, a liberal arts degree is more valuable today than ever before. While we have experienced breathtaking technological and industrial developments that have helped make us one of the most prosperous nations in the world, corporations are now also competing in a global marketplace. In response to this shifting landscape, corporations have become less hierarchical, and require employees who are generalists rather than specialists, who can cultivate the complex international relationships that will help them to compete internationally.

Who is better equipped than liberal arts majors—whose scope is the big picture, and whose sweep of study has trained them to understand and think critically about people, cultures, and society—to step in and fill the void?

So relax. Have a sense of humor about the mocking knocks on your degree, because they are rooted in myth. You are uniquely qualified for the changes taking shape. You will find a job—a good entry-level job, and not necessarily in the fast-food industry. (Although the fast-food sector is one of the fastest growing, with the top three chains alone offering hundreds of thousands of employees the opportunity to grow into management positions.)

Your job search is no more difficult than it is for any other major. It's just different. Furthermore, you don't need to agonize over making a perfect, lifetime decision. Your first job need not, and probably will not, have anything to do with what you studied. The first job is usually a learning experience, just one point on the horizon that helps you navigate toward your career.

You will also probably have more than one career in your

lifetime. Most people change careers at least three times in their lives. Some careers you will pursue purposefully. Others you will stumble into accidentally. Don't allow friends, family, or society to pressure you. Let the *pre*med, *pre*law, *pre*business students whose careers were seemingly *pre*determined from conception suffer from angst about Kaplan courses, LSATs, GPAs, and how much to bid for a chance to interview with each consulting and Big Six company that recruits on campus.

You are a liberal arts major, and you will pave your road to success as you go along. You understand that a degree is not a destiny, and that success is a journey, not a destination. You will be hired for who you are, not what your major was. Presumably, those are some of the reasons you chose to be a liberal arts major. Now is the time to continue building on what you have accomplished and confidently take the next step on your journey.

Just Point Me in the Right Direction

What is the next step on your journey, and how do you take it? What can you do with a liberal arts degree? Where do you look for information about different careers, companies, and jobs? Do you look for a job now, or can you wait? What are the entry-level jobs really like? What do companies look for in candidates? How do you network? How do you put together cover letters and résumés? How do you prepare for and conduct yourself on interviews?

Together, step-by-step, we will demystify the job-search process and provide perspective on the often conflicting, confusing, irrelevant, and sometimes erroneous information published by the so-called experts in hyped career guides where titles like "Résumés That Win Jobs!" sit on shelves next to "Résumés *Don't* Win Jobs!" We will uncover the simple truths about the job-search process, shatter myths about interviews, and seek to understand what companies are really looking for in candidates. We'll discuss common missteps and how to avoid them. Finally, we'll get an inside view of entry-level jobs in various industries and learn what the culture and the day-to-day responsibilities are really like. It's all basic, but the process is often made more complicated than it has to be.

I have worked in Human Resources for ten years, and have

been teaching communications courses to undergraduate students at New York University for fourteen years. During this time I have taught, interviewed, referred, rejected, hired, sometimes fired, counseled, and advised thousands of college students, mostly liberal arts majors. I've conducted career workshops and participated on career panels on college campuses across the country. One of the courses that I teach at NYU is called Interviewing Strategies. The class is a microcosm of graduating seniors across the country including everyone from body-pierced, black-clad artists to Michael Milken–wannabe business students.

These and other students I've met during my career all have something in common: they understand very little about transferring the skills they acquired in college to a successful job search. Students are frequently preoccupied with minutiae and focus on form rather than substance ("What's the right answer when a recruiter asks me why I want this job?" "Should I put my GPA on my résumé?" "What color paper should I use?" "How important is the career objective?").

The truth is, when it comes down to who gets the job and who doesn't, the decision is never about fonts, transcripts, or memorizing the correct answers to interview questions. It's about you—who and what kind of person you are and whether you can make a positive contribution to the company.

After several years of teaching and hiring recent graduates, it finally occurred to me that one of the reasons entry-level job seekers stumble through the job-search process is that while our educational institutions give students the tools necessary to succeed in the business world, they don't give them the tools necessary to conduct a successful job search to get *into* the business world, particularly liberal arts majors.

Each year our institutions drop hundreds of thousands of liberal arts majors onto the doorsteps of corporate America without preparing them to knock and get invited inside. Unfortunately for recent grads, educational institutions do not pump the money into their career development departments like they do other facilities. They do not require students to register for career counseling before they graduate, but they do impose other strict requirements for obtaining your diploma, such as turning in your cap and gown. Many career development departments, except in the smallest of colleges, aren't even equipped to handle every student because of limited resources. Furthermore, as you have probably already experienced, the resources and companies that are available through this department are geared predominantly toward business majors.

Even if you attend an exclusively liberal arts college, most of the companies that recruit on campus are the same banking, financial, insurance, consulting, and pharmaceutical companies that visit the business schools, and in which many liberal arts majors have no interest. This is due primarily to the varying needs of different companies and the nature of each industry's recruiting process. Many of the nonfinancial companies that appeal to liberal arts majors usually have neither the resources nor the need to recruit on campus. Therefore, many students avoid this department entirely, which is a mistake. The Career Development Center is still a valuable resource for liberal arts majors, and later we'll discuss further how to get the most out of this often underutilized department.

In the meantime, where do you turn for guidance? Well, if I have struck some responsive chord, if you feel I understand something about who you are—your questions and concerns— then perhaps you will have confidence in my ability to help. There is nothing profound about my philosophy, which is based on years of experience. It is remarkable in its simplicity. This is a candid, practical, and step-by-step approach to helping you to understand what is important in the process of choosing a career and looking for a job. We follow a time line and discuss each component of the job-search process at its simple, empirical truth. Each chapter builds on the principles discussed in the preceding ones, so don't selectively read chapters even if you think you are already familiar with the content. You don't know what you don't know, and you may miss something of value.

You are more prepared than you realize for your journey. Through your studies you know that the world is a delicate balance of colliding sociologies and ideologies, where effective communication can only result from an understanding of diverse cultures. That history can be seen in art through the brushstrokes of painters and in literature from the pens of writers.

This sweeping knowledge transfers to the workplace, where

there is an urgent need to understand and manage the dynamics of an increasingly diverse, multicultural workforce, and where the ability to communicate effectively and bring clarity to complex business material are two of the most important skills required for business success and career advancement.

So, the question put forth to liberal arts majors should not be "What can you do with *that* degree?" Rather, it is "What *can't* you do with that degree?"

THE
LIBERAL ARTS
ADVANTAGE

PART
ONE

Back to Basics

> In the movie **Bull Durham**, *a minor league baseball team is in the throes of its worst losing streak ever. To break the streak, the players abandon the fundamentals and resort to gimmicks. The pitcher tries wearing women's underwear, and the rest of the players put voodoo on their bats and gloves. Finally, the manager gets fed up with all of these gimmicks and reminds the team to stick to the basics. "Baseball is a simple game. You hit the ball. You throw the ball. You catch the ball."*

I was scanning the vast array of titles in the careers section of a bookstore one day and I was amazed at how flooded the market was with individual books deconstructing the job-search process into the most minute elements. Why would anyone need an entire book on writing a cover letter? Or a résumé, for that matter? There are even books solely dedicated to explaining how to dress for an interview! Now, it is true that many a fashion faux pas and Glamour Don't have been committed by job seekers. But an entire book? Hel-lo! Socks, shoes, shirt, tie, and suit for the men; substitute stockings and blouse for the women. Make sure the ensemble matches and is appropriate for business, and if you have any doubt, ask a store salesperson. Bingo! Ninety percent of the job seekers now know how to dress appropriately for an interview.

Intrigued, I delved further into the shelves and was struck by how the titles vie for attention: "99," "101," "301," "555" of the Best/Unique: Ways to Answer Interview Questions; Write Thank You Notes; Network; Answer Want Ads; Shake Hands," etc. There are "High Impact Résumés," "Perfect Résumés," "Knock 'em

Dead Résumés," "Killer Résumés." Next we'll have "Résumés That Kill People Who Reject Them!" I found similar books for cover letters with slightly less violent titles. "Now," "Hidden," "Top Secret," "Guerrilla," and "Zen Art" techniques help you find jobs, and "Parachute Coloring" and "Rainbow Building" techniques help you find yourself so you can find a job. Keep in mind that many of these books are written by people who write for a living. My favorites are the hip guides written by twentysomethings for twentysomethings because they claim to be able to "speak your language," but reduce every recent graduate to a Generation-X stereotype.

What does any of this have to do with a liberal arts graduate's search for guidance about different careers and conducting a successful job search? I understand the need to creatively market a title in a crowded marketplace, but landing an entry-level job is not about gimmicks, games, and guerrilla tactics. It is about preparation, a positive attitude, initiative, and maturity. It's about understanding who you are, what you want and need, and what employers want and need.

Some books say that *the first job is critical, it puts you on the track of success or failure, happiness or shattered dreams. If you don't get the job you want straight out of college, you will have great difficulty and settle for less in your career.* Now that's uplifting. Nothing like a little extra pressure when you're still searching for your first job. So, if you've already found your first job, and it didn't turn out to be exactly what you had hoped for, you might as well tattoo a big *L* on your forehead for LOSER!

I wonder what the following people would have to say about that first job advice: *Michael Ovitz,* one of the most powerful Hollywood agents, started out in the mailroom: *Alan Greenspan,* chairman of the Federal Reserve, toured with a dance band, playing clarinet and saxophone; *Tom Clancy* is a former insurance agent; *Billy Crystal* was a substitute teacher; *Jay Leno* was a Rolls Royce auto mechanic.

"I'll Have a Part-skim Triple-Mocha Double-Latte Frappa Cappuccino"

As I've stated, the huge demand for career guidance is replenished with each graduating class partly due to our educational system. Liberal arts majors, feeling disadvantaged in their job search and alarmed by statistics that suggest they are doomed to the unemployment line, flock to career guides for advice and a new, innovative approach to give them a competitive edge. Career gurus oblige and offer unique, *off-the-wall* techniques many students blindly follow. Frequently the results aren't pretty, with many candidates unnecessarily shooting themselves in the foot.

Instead of contributing to the hype, we're discussing basics. Hiring managers and human resources professionals across the country know how frustrating it is to interview a parade of applicants who haven't been advised or who are misguided by career books that overcomplicate the process. However, they never despair. For you, finding the right job—any job—can be difficult. For them, spotting the right candidate is very easy.

They know that eventually someone will walk through the door confidently but not aggressively, smile, look them in the eye, and say earnestly, "I'm a recent liberal arts graduate and I am prepared for a career in this field. I'm intelligent, mature, eager, and have a positive attitude. I've researched this industry and your company, and I know what to expect in an entry-level position. Let me tell you what I've accomplished thus far, how it demonstrates my various skills, character, initiative, and how my strengths relate to this job. I get along well in groups because of my strong interpersonal skills, and I can also work independently. I will represent the company well and be an overall asset."

That's not being a cookie-cutter candidate, a clone without individuality. It's actually novel. It demonstrates an understanding of the process and not just what *you* want and need, but what the *employer* wants and needs.

It's really basic, but unfortunately, it doesn't happen often enough. Your liberal arts degree is your advantage. You are prepared. Trust that your individuality will come through without gimmicks. Make it easy for the employer, who will appreciate and hire you for it. Stick to the basics, which never went out of style for getting a job. Someone just needs to remind you that there was a time when coffee was just coffee and ordering a cup didn't require an illustrated dictionary and an ATM withdrawal.

Basic Business Essentials

Before you get too confident about your readiness to enter the business world, you should know that I've encountered too many liberal arts majors who wait until their senior year to begin thinking about career preparation, only to find they still need to develop a few skills essential for being competitive in the job market. Whether you are a freshman or recent grad, it's never too early or too late to acquire basic business skills appropriate to any career.

Many liberal arts majors spend their entire college careers avoiding business classes, business students, the business section of newspapers, anything having to do with business, leaving them with an incomplete preparation for, and understanding of, the issues which form and transform the workplace and the world.

I'm not suggesting that you need the business acumen of an economist or a financial analyst, but if you do not already understand the basic principles of business, finance, and accounting, then you should brush up by taking a few introductory classes. If you've already graduated, there are numerous continuing education classes, one-day seminars, and books available that can acquaint you with business issues and terminology. Take basic accounting, finance, and economics courses. Learn how the stock market works, how to read a balance sheet, and what a fiscal year is. You should also read the business section of the newspaper and one of the weekly business newsmagazines regularly. Every industry from banking and finance to arts and entertainment is a business. Therefore, an understanding and awareness of the business world in which you intend to work is essential for your job search and career. Moreover, the knowledge is just as essential to have in your personal life, which everyone realizes the first time they have to prepare their taxes, rent an apartment, and pay their bills on an entry-level salary.

Employers also prefer candidates who have some experience working in an office environment. There are certain basic office procedures and accepted codes of conduct that you can pick up just by osmosis. Managers are frequently shocked by recent graduates who conduct themselves immaturely, can't answer phones or take messages properly, don't know how to format a simple business letter, and don't know any better than to barge into someone's office when the door is closed.

While lifeguarding, waiting tables, and cashiering are honest jobs that help pay the bills and can teach you many valuable skills that you can apply to an office environment, there is no substitute for the experience of actually working in an office. So, if you're still in college, make sure you spend at least one semester, break, or summer working in an office.

Obviously, gaining experience in a field that you might pursue after graduation is ideal. However, if you don't know what you want to do, or don't even want to think about it yet, then just work in any office so that you can at least experience the culture and learn basic office skills. If you've spent your entire college career locked inside the hallowed halls of academia and have never worked in an office, then put down this book and head straight to a temporary employment agency. Temp for a week. Do anything—file, answer phones—just get inside an office and make sure you don't have an allergic reaction to the experience before you begin your job search. Later, we'll discuss how temporary employment can also be one of the most effective means for conducting your job search.

Make sure you stay current with changes in technology. You don't have to be a "techie," but being computer savvy—knowing how to surf the Net and use spreadsheets and advanced word-processing applications—will enhance your productivity, the quality of your work, and therefore your value and marketability. Again, if you have the opportunity to upgrade your skills in school, take advantage of it. If not, then make the investment to do it on your own. It will be worth it not only because the skills are marketable but also because it demonstrates initiative you can refer to during an interview.

Finally, do you know what consistently ranks as people's greatest fear? Public speaking. The thought of speaking in front of a crowd, whether in a social setting like a party, or at work in front of a board of directors, is absolutely terrifying for most people. Most people avoid it at all costs, and many people who are forced to speak publicly do not do it well. Therefore, the ability to communicate confidently and effectively in this manner is an invaluable asset for getting ahead in business. Employees who are skilled at encouraging, explaining, motivating, and articulating goals, and who volunteer to accept assignments with a high degree of visibility through public speaking, tend to advance to more responsible positions in management. So take a speech class, improve your public speaking ability, and know that you possess an invaluable skill that most professionals do not have.

CHAPTER TWO —————

Do What You Are

> Live all you can; it's a mistake not to.
> It doesn't so much matter what you do in particular, so
> long as you have had your life.
> If you haven't had that what have you had? . . .
>
> —Henry James

Time Off

Four years of college: four years of midterms and finals, endless nights studying and partying, battling with financial aid, forging friendships and relationships. Isn't it exhausting just thinking about how much you compressed into those four years? Do you need a break? Do you really want to start working right after graduation? Students often ask if they will be disadvantaged in any way by delaying their job search. Is one time of year better than another to look for a job? Will companies think they aren't ambitious because they didn't look for a job right away?

My response is always the same: If you have a burning desire to backpack across Europe for two months, experiencing the cultures and people you studied, exploring museums and seeing in person the artwork and sights you only experienced through photographs; or to work on the environment in Alaska or the rain forests; bicycle cross-country; teach inner-city youths; build huts in Botswana; or just be a beach bum in Bermuda; *then do it now!* It's not as if jobs are only available in the month you graduate. While recruiting for training programs may occur at specific times during the year, entry-level positions in most industries are available year-round.

You will always be able to look for a job, but you may never again have the opportunity to take as much time off as you want to do whatever you desire until you retire. That may be FORTY YEARS from now. By then, the inspiration and romanticism will be gone, and it's just not the same. Wild adventures will entail waiting in the buffet line on a seven-day Carnival Cruise, or playing the slots in Atlantic City or shuffleboard at the nursing home.

If you're deep in debt from college tuition and worried about money, another few thousand isn't going to make a difference. Student loans can be deferred, but your youth can't. Don't feel pressured if your friends have jobs or your parents think you should start working immediately. This is your life. Your friends with jobs will envy you and your parents will still love you. If you really want or need to take this time off, and you don't, you'll regret it.

Furthermore, taking time off isn't just about letting loose or living out impractical fantasies. It can also be beneficial to your job search. Generally, employers feel that when students expand their horizons by pursuing varied interests, whether at home or abroad, it demonstrates initiative and a level of maturity that may better prepare them for the work environment. Whether or not your parents buy into that rationale enough to help you finance your little sabbatical is another story!

Don't Be a Statistic

Before you can mount an effective job search, you must identify the job or industry you would like to pursue. Often, students turn to yearly employment outlook reports for direction. They research employment statistics and analyze the surveys on the best and worst cities for jobs, occupations projected for growth, the state of the job market, and average starting salaries. However, these reports are subjective and are based on forecasts, opinions, and data that can be interpreted in many different ways. For instance, two different 1997 surveys that listed the top fifteen

U.S. cities for job growth had only five cities in common. Two other surveys of the top ten jobs for career growth had only four in common.

The Department of Labor forecasts that in the next five years there will be an average of 1.4 million new graduates each year, and only 1.1 million new jobs. But is the job market really grim? Not really, because these numbers are misleading. It's not as if each year on June 1, 1.4 million graduates will descend upon the workforce, competing for interviews and jobs and leaving 300,000 other grads in the cold. The economy and job market aren't static. There are constant turnovers and shifts in the workforce that make trying to draw rational and relevant conclusions from these numbers impossible. Most of the information, whether geared to college grads or not, is irrelevant, especially at this point in your career. (Unless, of course, you had your sights set on becoming an electronic pagination systems worker, which, according to the surveys, is predicted to be one of the fastest-growing occupations of the next ten years.)

Here's all you need to know at this point in your career about the job market: There will always be jobs available in just about any industry college grads could be interested in. Some industries always have been, and always will be, tougher to break into than others, regardless of the job market. The competition for jobs in the communications/arts fields such as television, radio, film, advertising, publishing, public relations, journalism, and fashion is always tough because they are perceived as the "creative" or "glamour" industries. As you might expect, there is less competition for jobs in engineering, social services, and health care.

Your career choice should be based on what is important to you, not on statistics or on what other people want or think you should do.

Remember, you will spend more time working than you spend doing any other single activity in your life. A typical entry-level person works, conservatively, nine to ten hours a day. Depending on the industry it could be much more, but rarely is it less. When you add getting ready for work and travel time to and from work, you have approximately twelve hours of every day dedicated to some work-related activity. Sleeping takes up the second most amount of time in a twenty-four-hour period;

figure another seven hours. That's nineteen of every twenty-four hours, nearly 80 percent of your day, dedicated to work and sleeping! Which only leaves five hours for eating, chores, working out, television, reading, spending time with a significant other (which could be a pet since you obviously won't have time for a human relationship) and anything else you can cram in. Depressing? Only if you don't enjoy your work. If you had to choose a recreational activity you would do every single day, you wouldn't choose something you didn't look forward to and didn't enjoy. Apply the same principle to your work.

If you still don't know what you want to do, Part Two of this book provides an overview of interesting industries, career paths, and typical jobs. However, there is no substitute for first-hand experience. Working as an intern or temp in the field you might be interested in allows you to make a truly informed decision.

Salary

In The Godfather Part 2, *Al Pacino's niece and her fiancé ask him for his blessing for them to wed. Al Pacino asks the young man what he studies in college. When the fiancé replies, "Liberal arts," Al Pacino laughs and asks, "How do you expect to support my niece on liberal arts?" The fiancé replies, "I'm a major stockholder in my family's business."*

It is a myth that liberal arts majors are doomed to a life of abject poverty unless they are heirs to an inheritance. Liberal arts majors can be found at every level of corporations in every field. According to *Fortune* magazine, nearly one-third of all CEOs majored in liberal arts. Typical salary ranges for some industries are lower than others. And while it is true that the industries liberal arts majors are generally attracted to fall at the low end of the spectrum, your career choice should not be based on money. However, you should be familiar with the typical salary ranges in the careers you are considering so that your expectations are realistic. Average starting salaries in communications, arts, and social services typically range from $18,000 to $22,000 per year.

Starting salaries for business and engineering jobs usually range from $25,000 to $35,000 per year.

Are you going to choose a profession because of starting salaries, or how much you could earn after five or ten years? Does the fact that investment bankers can earn more money in one year than schoolteachers earn in ten motivate you to become an investment banker? Does the fact that advertising executives earn more than journalists motivate you to switch fields?

Most of you probably know what types of professions interest you and where you would fit in. Sometimes outside influences make you doubt the direction your head and heart say to take. Follow your passion. Do what you are.

Location, Location, Location

They say there are three keys to opening a successful business—location, location, location! Deciding where you want to work is just as important as deciding what you want to do. Here again, statistics are only as useful as you make them. Obviously, you have to make sure your chosen profession is available where you want to live or you will have to choose a different profession or place to live. If you want to work in film, your career isn't going to go very far in Boise, Idaho. However, if you want to live in Boise, it helps to know that Boise ranks among the top five cities for job growth in the high-tech and retail industries.

While few industries are located in just one city or region of the country, there are some careers that might require you to temporarily live somewhere you'd prefer not to. Broadcast journalism is one example. It is so difficult to break into broadcasting that in order to get a start, you almost always have to go wherever the job is, usually in a small market to start. In order to build your career, you may have to follow jobs to increasingly larger markets, which may lead you through cities that aren't your preference until you reach one that is.

When deciding where to live, it's important to consider whether or not there are competing companies in that city. That is, if you want to work in advertising, are there only one or two advertising agencies in that city? The more competing companies in that city, the better it is for you, not only for opportunities to start out but for building your career. Companies competing for the same business are also competing for the same talent interested in the business. Your marketability is important leverage. If your company is the only game in town, there is less concern that they will lose you to the competition.

A perfect example of this is advertising sales in magazine publishing. This can be a lucrative, exciting profession with tremendous career growth. The publisher of a magazine often ascends from the sales ranks. Top sales representatives for national magazines can earn upward of $100,000 annually. Most of the major national consumer magazines are based in New York City, and competition for sales talent can be fierce. It is not uncommon for companies to make copies of the competition's mastheads and lists of every employee. Each company keeps charts of the competition's personnel like television executives tracking each network's weekly programming. Sales reps are always trying to move up in account base and prestige in the magazine they represent. Obviously, that kind of environment presents many more career opportunities than would a city that has only one or two publications.

Keep in mind that work may be what you do twelve hours per day, but where you live is home twenty-four hours a day. It's important that you like the people, nightlife, culture, and entertainment (not to mention climate), that the city offers diversions outside of work that interest you.

Finally, take into consideration friends and family. MCI may be as close as you want to get to your family, or you may want to be closer. Starting a new job is tough enough. Doing it by yourself in a strange city can be very lonesome. I've seen many recent graduates, much to their own surprise, return home to a support system and find work in more familiar surroundings.

CHAPTER THREE

The Résumé

In the movie Good Morning Vietnam, *Robin Williams plays an army radio broadcaster who unknowingly befriends a North Vietnamese spy. After having a series of insubordinate run-ins with his superiors, accidentally releasing classified information, becoming an unwitting accomplice in bombings, and finally being detected while cavorting with the enemy, Williams's character, in disbelief, runs down this list of dubious accomplishments, then screams, "This is not going to look good on a résumé!"*

Before you can actively pursue a position, you must create the workhorse of your job search: the résumé. More has been written about this single document than about every other part of the job search combined. The subject of much debate, résumés have inspired dozens of books with conflicting advice about appropriate style, format, and content.

With so much confusion among the "experts," how are job seekers supposed to know how to tackle the daunting task of compressing their experience, education and skills onto one page?

You do not begin preparing a résumé when you decide to look for a job. You have been preparing a résumé throughout your entire life. All of your experiences have helped shape the person you are. However, at this point in your career, only what you've accomplished since your freshman year of college is relevant for your résumé.

All of your work, experience, skills, activities, honors, and accomplishments (or lack thereof) have helped shape your résumé. But there isn't much room to work with: just one 8½ × 11 sheet of paper—that precious canvas on which to paint your likeness with words and experiences. What does your résumé say about you? How does it say it?

The résumé is the first opportunity to show off your liberal arts degree. You didn't spend your four years crunching numbers; you studied the world, cultures, people, politics, history, religion, literature. You are prepared to enter the global marketplace because that is what you studied. Employers are not looking for specific majors, especially for entry-level positions. They're looking at the scope of your accomplishments, activities, experience, and skills. They are looking for dimension and character. How is that reflected in your résumé? What kind of personality does your résumé have? What kind do you have? The résumé allows employers a glimpse into who you are.

It is an important tool for marketing yourself and your credentials. A well-prepared résumé can help unlock doors. However, the best résumés cannot get anyone a job. Only you can do that. Many new graduates do not grasp that. They spend days agonizing over details such as, Do I put my name in bold caps in the center or to the left? What color paper should I use? How large should the font be? Which font type? Do I include my GPA or not? SAT scores or not? They take special care to make their résumés look perfectly groomed and professional. If only they took as much care with the other aspects of the job search.

For many new grads, the act of creating and mailing their résumé is a milestone. It is your unofficial coming-out party. For the past four years you have been kept under wraps in preparation for this major event. Now, your life, represented by one precious piece of paper, is carefully sealed in an envelope. Your mind retraces every step of its preparation as you let it slowly slip from your fingertips into the mailbox with slight apprehension. For one brief, panic-stricken moment, you are sure you must have missed some obvious mistake. As it slides down the chute, you quickly recover, reassured that you took great care in its preparation. How you will be received is now out of your hands. You sit back, and wait . . .

Liaison?

DAY ONE: The mail doesn't work that fast. It's still winding its way through the post office. I did put a stamp on it, didn't I?

DAY TWO: Still too early. Better check the answering machine to make sure it's working, just in case.

DAY THREE: Surely today is the day. How should I answer the pone if they call? "Hello, may I speak with Michael please?" You've got him! No, you idiot. This is he. Don't sound too eager. Your pulse quickens each time the phone rings. Wow, that was quick, they must have been really impressed. All false alarms. It's as if the phone knows it's playing with my emotions.

DAY FOUR: You go out because you need some air. When you return, three messages. You can barely breathe as each beep sounds. Your mother calling to see if they called yet. Your mother calling again to see where you are. Your mother calling a third time to see why you haven't returned her first two phone calls. They probably called when she was calling and the machine couldn't pick up so now your entire career is ruined! I'll have to call them. Tell them I just found out my machine is broken, and I just wanted to check to see if they were trying to reach me. No, that's too transparent. I'll wait until Monday.

DAY SEVEN: Monday's not a good day to call. Perhaps they collected all of the résumés and brought them home over the weekend. The manager will probably come in today and show mine to everyone. (You pull out a copy of your résumé.)

They are probably standing around admiring it, noticing the linen white, extra-heavy bond paper I used. I mailed in an 8½ × 11 envelope so that it wouldn't crease. I wonder if they appreciate my fine choice of fonts, Ariel, 10-point. Is it my GPA that is wowing them, or making dean's list every semester? I'm especially proud of the Interests Section. What an erudite young man, they must be saying. Loves to travel, play chess, opera, reading, and enjoys equestrian activities! How accommodating I am—References Available Upon Request. Surely with such a résumé, references will not be necessary. I wonder if they are impressed with my command of the language, and those action verbs: implemented, orchestrated, directed. Look at how deftly I tossed in that word, Liason. Liason with senior management . . . Liason? Why does that look funny? Liason. That is how it's spelled, isn't it? Liason, laison, liason. L-i-a- . . . **i** . . **I? I? I don't believe it!!!** How could that happen?! Well, I didn't want to work for that company, anyway . . . or the other twenty-five I just sent my résumé to. Four years of hard work and accomplishments down the drain!

Many new grads are obsessive-compulsive about every detail of a résumé's style. The only thing important about the style and format is that it doesn't interfere with its essential ability to work for you. Understanding what happens to your résumé after it is sent out, and how it is used by employers, will help put its preparation into perspective and help you quickly and easily create one for any job without going through a torturous process.

Behind the Scenes

When you send your résumé to a company, let's say in response to a job posted at school or advertised in the newspaper, it does not receive the same care and attention it did when you created it. No one is waiting around for the mail to come, eagerly sorting through it until they come upon your envelope with your résumé neatly tucked inside. There is no fanfare, drumroll, or ceremonial opening of the envelope. It is like the hundred other pieces of mail: ripped open by an assistant, stamped RECEIVED with a date, and put in a pile with every other résumé received that week.

The person in the human resources department responsible for going through that pile, which could include 50 to 100 résumés for the same position, is probably a recruiter, a very busy individual under a lot of pressure. This isn't the only position they are working to fill. There could be dozens of openings in various departments and at different levels for which they are recruiting. Hundreds of résumés each week and month; thousands of résumés each year.

Hiring managers want their positions filled immediately and are waiting to see either résumés or candidates that the recruiter has prescreened. Recruiters often don't have the time to look at every résumé, let alone read them. So if the pile is big, their first goal is to reduce the stack by quick scanning into two smaller piles—IN or OUT. On the first pass, ten seconds per résumé, that's it. Sometimes less. Clean, neat, professional looking, enough white space—IN. Sloppy, white-out, typewritten, coffee stains, pink—OUT. Those are common.

The truly horrendous résumés are saved for a good laugh. A photo impression of the sender in the upper right-hand corner waving hello. Words cut out from magazines and pasted to the page like a ransom note. Or, to compensate for four years of classes but little or no work experience or activities, triple-spaced résumés in 24-point type.

If all of this seems obvious to you, then you are ahead of the game because all of the above résumé "types" are actual résumés I've seen over the years from liberal arts degreed college grads entering the job market.

The Four Ws

Now that the pile has been reduced, if your résumé made the cut, it will be reviewed for thirty to sixty seconds on the second pass. Knowing what the person screening the résumé is looking for in those thirty to sixty seconds, and providing it, will help your résumé make the final cut. Think of your résumé as the lead paragraph of a news article: *who, what, where, when.* The why and how are for the cover letter and interview, which we will get to in later chapters.

The person reviewing your résumé doesn't have the time or the interest to decipher your résumé. So the layout has to be simple and uniform, not fancy. They have read thousands of résumés and have developed a system for reviewing them.

Don't tinker with your résumé to make it stand out; no wacky colors, creative, maze-like layouts, odd-sized paper, etc. Don't give them a reason to eliminate your résumé. They want a wrench, so give them a wrench—not a screwdriver that also functions as a wrench if they take the time to read the instructions. They won't.

Step-by-Step Résumé

There are three basic types of résumés: *chronological, functional,* and *combination.* Chronological résumés list experience in reverse order: the most recent at the top, working backward. Functional résumés enable you to group skills and information at the top rather than listing job responsibilities at each place worked. Combination résumés feature elements of both. They allow you to group relevant experiences and job responsibilities related to the job or industry to which you are applying.

Many employers find functional résumés annoying and unimpressive. The list of skills and summary statements are not directly related to specific jobs and activities where the skills were acquired. Students are often told to use this format when they have little related experience. In most cases, it is better to use either a chronological or combination résumé. Actually, you will need both types, and if you are interviewing for positions in different industries, you may need to create more than one combination résumé. Intimidated? Don't be. It's very easy to do. You don't need to spend money on a résumé-writing software package or résumé-writing service. You can do it yourself. You just need a word processor, a little guidance, and a little time.

Before we begin, let's resolve one lengthy debate—make it only one page. End of discussion. Now you know how much room you have to work with. There is not much you can do about the upper-third portion of your résumé: name, address, telephone number, and education. So, what we're really talking about is what to put on the remaining two-thirds of the page. That isn't a lot of room to describe four years of achievements, so you have to use it wisely. The first step is not to obsess over what is relevant and how to cram it into the remaining few inches of space. The first step is to create your personal profile—a list of everything you've accomplished over the past four years, organized by category.

Don't worry about what you think is relevant, how long it is, or how you say it—just get everything down on paper, but take your time. Four years is a long time and you've probably done a lot. Use the following outline as a guide for organizing your information, and remember, for the purpose of this exercise *everything* is relevant: lifeguarding, juggling, frat-house cookie sale, bike-a-thon, crossword puzzle hobby, *everything*.

  I. Education
 II. Work Experience
III. Skills
IV. Activities
 V. Honors/Awards
VI. Interests

Once you've created your personal profile, you then have a database of information from which you can quickly and easily

Jessica Cunningham Personal Profile

EXPERIENCE
Summer Internship ABC Broadcasting 6/96–9/96
Typed, filed, answered phones, sorted mail, made copies
Summer 6/95–9/95: Waitress and Bartender at Sparky's
Spring Semester 2/95–4/95: part-time at local newspaper—
general clerical
Summer 6/94–7/94: Lifeguard
Fall Semester 10/94–12/94: part-time at local magazine—
general clerical

EDUCATION
B.A. History
Liberal Arts University
Rochester, MN—May 97

Semester abroad to study French
Sorbonne, Paris, France

HONORS
Dean's list every semester
Journalism award for Feature Writing

ACTIVITIES
Volunteer at school radio station two hours per week
Volunteer at school newspaper two hours per week
Sorority house fund-raiser
Community recycling program
Swim team
Student government

SKILLS
Word 6.0; Mac photoshop; fluent French and Italian; excellent
writing; public speaking

INTERESTS
Reading, current events, hiking, fishing

prepare a chronological résumé and different combination résumés targeted specifically for each different job. Let's create a personal profile of a typical liberal arts grad, and from it create a chronological and combination résumé (see opposite page).

The Great Résumé Debate

Before we create sample résumés, we should first clear up a few points. Since the résumé is often the first impression an employer has of you, it should be pristine. No one disputes that. But there are seemingly endless debates over irrelevant stylistic and content points that border on the absurd. There are also many pet peeves employers have about common résumé mistakes that you should be aware of.

Title

What title? Do you think that there is anyone out there who doesn't know that they are looking at a résumé? Don't put *résumé* at the top of your résumé. Even worse is *professional profile* or *curriculum vitae*—unless you are an education professional with years of experience in the industry. Don't get cute; just your name on top will do.

Address and Telephone Number

Don't make the employer search high and low for your whereabouts. If you are in transition, you can have two addresses and phone numbers: one temporary, the other permanent. Just make sure that an employer can leave a message any time of day at whatever phone number you provide. You will most likely miss an opportunity if someone calls and cannot leave a message. (However, while beepers seem to have become a fashion accessory, listing a beeper number is not only going overboard, it may raise some concerns about your extracurricular activities.)

Paper

Do not use copy machine paper and do not use cover stock that barely folds. Choose a good quality stock that lies flat on the table and doesn't curl up at the ends. Just walk into any stationery store or copy center and ask for résumé paper, and they will show you a selection in a vast array of colors.

Color

Any shade of white: off-white, eggshell, linen-white, ivory, etc.—whatever turns you on, it doesn't matter, just as long as it is in the white family. Every other color is unprofessional and doesn't help the applicant gain an edge in securing an interview. In some cases, the reverse is true, and their résumés aren't considered because of the poor judgment displayed in choosing that color. Get blank sheets and matching envelopes so that you can prepare matching cover letters and send out a professional application.

Font

Stick to easy-to-read, clean typefaces like Ariel or Times New Roman. And don't go crazy with bold, italics, and underline. The most effective résumé is one that is aesthetically inviting to look at and read. Going overboard with creative fonts or boldfacing and italicizing everything but the dates is like wearing a striped shirt with a polka dot tie and a plaid jacket (it hurts my eyes just to write that). Less is more became a cliché for a reason.

Career Objective

The career objective inspires passionate debate. Let's put an end to it right here. It's a waste of time and precious space on your résumé. Again: A waste of time and precious space on your résumé. Leave it off. Why? Because your résumé is supposed to reflect what you have accomplished, not what you want. As we have discussed, there is so little room on the résumé to describe your accomplishments, you can't waste it on trivial information that they should have learned by other means. One popular career guide on the market suggests that the following would be an effective career objective: "My objective is to secure an entry-level position with a major corporation offering opportunities for growth and advancement." This banal statement means absolutely nothing. Did you think the employer might get confused without it and think that you were applying for some dead-end job with no opportunity for growth and advancement?

The objective serves no purpose other than to overstate the obvious and waste space that could be used for your experience, skills, honors, activities—things that matter. One recent grad took that book's advice a step farther. Career objective: "To utilize my God-given creative talents in an entry-level position for a progressive company that will allow me to learn and grow." Thank you for playing, we have some lovely parting gifts for you. Some suggest that your career objective should be specific: "To secure an entry-level position in account management for an advertising agency." This type of objective can limit your employment opportunities. When applying for an entry-level job, what you really want is to get your foot in the door. Being focused is fine, but don't be myopic and close yourself off to other positions that you would have considered if you had only known about them. With this objective, an employer may not bother considering you for anything other than what you have so specifically stated. The cover letter that accompanies your résumé will explain what it is that you are looking for.

GPA/SAT Scores

I am sorry to be the one to break this to you, or you may find this a great relief, but no one cares about your GPA or SAT scores. OK? Only graduate and professional schools look at GPAs and test scores. Employers don't care. Why then, you may ask, do certain campus recruiters establish a minimum GPA for students who wish to interview? Because they need some mechanism for controlling the number of résumés they will receive and have to read. They may not publicly admit this, but it's true.

The GPA is so arbitrary and subjective that it has been rendered almost meaningless. One has to take into account too many variables for a GPA to have any significance. How difficult is the institution, the course work, the professors? How many other activities was the student involved in? Did they work while in college? If you have a 4.0 but spent the entire four years buried in books and nothing else, that's a problem. If you still want to put your GPA on your résumé, go ahead; it won't hurt as long as it is sterling—3.5 and above. Leave off the SATs even if you did score 1600.

Dates

A common pet peeve among employers is applicants who leave out dates or provide incomplete and often misleading dates.

When providing dates, always include month and year, but leave out the day, e.g., May 1995 or 5/95. I prefer spelling out the month because I think it looks better, but it doesn't matter. Never put just the year, e.g., 1995, or 1995–1996. Both suggest that the date applies to a full year. However, 1995–1996 could be as short as two days: 12/31/95 to 1/1/96, or it could be as long as two years: 1/1/95 to 12/31/96. When an applicant leaves out the months, it makes the employer suspicious because it usually means the person is trying to hide something or make the experience look longer than it really was.

Employers resent having to guess and work hard to establish a time line. This is a common ploy of someone who has been in the workforce but has a spotty employment history and is trying to cover gaps or short-lived employment. It is a trick that always fails, and for a recent graduate it is totally unnecessary. The nature of employment for college students is sporadic, fit around school schedules, breaks, and summers. It is expected that you will have gaps and short-term jobs, so there is no need to try to hide it.

The only time you do not have to provide the month and year is if you have held several short-term or part-time jobs during the same time frame. For example, let's say that one summer you waited tables for a few weeks at home, then spent the next two months at your summer home where you alternated between lifeguarding, waiting tables, and tending bar part-time. In that case you could keep it simple and just lump all of those jobs together under the same dates, e.g., 6/96 to 9/96, or you could just say Summer 1996, without having to give the specific weeks for each job. Everyone understands the nature of summer work.

Summary Statement/Qualifications

This is also used primarily on functional résumés. Summary statements that appear at the top of some résumés such as "I have excellent writing ability and can interact well with others. I have taken on leadership roles in school and work, and have successfully completed complex projects under deadline pressure" are frankly annoying because there isn't any way to match the skills with the specific jobs and activities listed on the résumé. It is better to list the responsibilities and skills acquired under each job or activity rather than summarizing everything at the top.

Experience

Students tend to fall into two extremes when describing their responsibilities in a particular job. At one extreme, they may say "general clerical duties" or just "typing, filing, answer phones, etc." Almost every entry-level or secretarial job could be reduced to these routine tasks. But give yourself a little credit. Most job responsibilities can be expanded to provide a more descriptive picture of what the nature of the work was, thereby lending the résumé a little more substance. This does not mean that you have a license to hyperbolize or worse, the cardinal sin of all résumés, lie. Never ever lie on your résumé. Moral issues aside, there is no way to recover credibility if you are caught lying. And everyone sees through such hyperbole as "Increased profits by providing service efficiently and expeditiously, thereby creating quick turnover and maximum value out of the tables in my station for a high-volume food service establishment." Get over it—you were a waitress, so just say that. It's hard work, and anyone who has ever worked in a restaurant knows that. It requires organizational and interpersonal skills and demonstrates an ability to work under pressure, all of which are transferable to an office environment. But no matter how you slice it, you were waiting tables.

Spelling

A typo on your résumé isn't so much a pet peeve as it is a disqualifier. You'd be surprised how many résumés have spelling errors or other mistakes, which frequently aren't caught by the person reviewing the résumé. Don't take the chance. Your spell-checking program isn't enough, because even though it may catch misspellings, it won't catch *repeat repeat* words, or if *your* using the wrong word. Foolproof proofreading is first using spell-check to catch the obvious mistakes, then reading your résumé both forward and backward.

The reason reading backward is effective is because when you are familiar with the flow of the text, your mind often doesn't read what is there, but what it thinks should be there and what you intended to say. Try reciting the alphabet backward. Your mind has to stop at each letter to make sure it is correct. Finally, have someone with a fresh eye read it. This may seem excessive, but too often I have seen résumés from bright recent graduates rejected because they didn't put in a few extra minutes to make sure they were perfect. Employers feel that if you were sloppy with your résumé, you wouldn't be any more careful with the work you produced and how you represented the company. Makes sense, right?

Verb Tense

When describing work or activities that you are currently doing, use the present tense: "Prepare reports, organize meetings, direct customers," etc. When you are describing work that you did previously but are no longer doing, use past tense: "Prepared reports, organized meetings, directed customers," etc. Be consistent.

How Far Back?

No one cares that you walked when you were nine months old or that you won the spelling bee in the tenth grade, except maybe your mother. The general rule of thumb is that precollege achievements are irrelevant unless you're only in your first or second year of college. However, achievements or work that are precollege but extraordinary in some way can be included. For example, recently there was a high school student who won a national science contest for inventing a computer chip that was faster than the ones used by computer manufacturers today. That would be relevant. Also, there are several high schools that are nationally recognized in areas such as the arts and sciences. In that case, it would be worthwhile to note your attendance on your résumé if you were pursuing a job in that field.

Skills

This is not the place to list your dubious frat or sorority house skills that won you accolades on campus. Generally included here are your computer and foreign language skills. Unless you qualify your degree of proficiency with a specific software, it will be assumed that you can handle at least the routine functions. The most common pitfall here is foreign languages. Don't misrepresent your language ability. If you are less than fluent, indicate that by writing "working knowledge," "written ability," or "conversational." However, if you can't get beyond, for example, *arroz con pollo,* leave it off altogether.

Personal History

Another favorite pet peeve: While you can make the analogy that the interview is like a first date, your résumé is not a personal ad. It is a summary of your accomplishments. Information such as your weight, height, age, or marital status makes employers cringe. Various laws prohibit employers from discriminating based on this information. Leave it off unless you are an actor and it appears on the back of your headshot.

Interests

This section is not the place to reveal bizarre fetishes or your predilection for tattooing and body-piercing. Avoid controversy. Include things you like to do in your spare time. These can often provide important icebreakers during interviews and create common ground to begin discussions. Whatever you do, do not put things that "look good" on your résumé, but about which you know very little or nothing. I was very interested in one applicant whose interests seemed to mirror many of my own. When I questioned him about one of them, chess, he looked at me like a deer in headlights. He stuttered, "Oh, I never really played, I am just interested in learning the game." His other interests became suspect at that point, and with very little probing he revealed a similar lack of knowledge. It's painful to watch applicants turn several shades of red and self-destruct like that.

References

By now everyone knows that references are *available upon request.* In my many years at this, I have never encountered an applicant who denied a request for references. Since résumé space is so limited, you can leave this off and use that line for something more important and illuminating. Instead, prepare a separate sheet with the names, addresses, and telephone numbers of individuals who have agreed to provide a reference for you. Alert them ahead of time that an employer may be calling.

Overall

Your pride in your accomplishments should come through on your résumé. The entire page should be consistent and uniform with plenty of white space. It must not look text dense; otherwise a reviewer won't want to even look at it, much less read it. The problem with the advice that says you should be creative with your résumé so that it will stand out from the crowd is that the creativity is misplaced. You can be creative in your job search to help your résumé get noticed, but once you get their attention, you want your résumé to reflect your professional image.

A publicist who wanted to work in the publicity department of a sports magazine sent her résumé wrapped around a baseball. The ball had her name, address, and telephone number on it, and a poem: "I can pitch a client with creative spin—if you want a good catch just call me in!" Her résumé got noticed. They saw that she had excellent experience and called her for an interview. However, despite her creative approach, she didn't interview well, and didn't get the job. There you go.

Now that you know what information employers are looking for, how quickly they need to get it, and how to avoid common mistakes, you can easily create your own résumé. The following résumé template provides a basic format that allows you to plug in specific information from your personal profile and quickly create a chronological résumé. The format can also be modified to create combination résumés that are targeted for specific jobs.

Chronological Résumé

YOUR NAME
Street Address
City, State, Zip Code
Phone Number

EDUCATION
Your College Name, City & State
Name of Your Degree, Year
Major/Minor

EXPERIENCE

COMPANY NAME, CITY & STATE   DATE
JOB TITLE
- An accomplishment from this job, illustrating a skill needed in the new job
- An accomplishment from this job, illustrating a skill needed in the new job
- An accomplishment from this job, illustrating a skill needed in the new job

COMPANY NAME, CITY & STATE   DATE
JOB TITLE
- An accomplishment from this job, illustrating a skill needed in the new job
- An accomplishment from this job, illustrating a skill needed in the new job
- An accomplishment from this job, illustrating a skill needed in the new job

ACTIVITIES
School or Community Activity   Date
School or Community Activity   Date
School or Community Activity   Date

SKILLS
Computer Skills
Foreign Languages
Writing Skills

Combination Résumé

YOUR NAME
Street Address
City, State, Zip Code
Phone Number

EDUCATION
Your College Name, City & State
Name of Your Degree, Year
Major/Minor

RELEVANT EXPERIENCE
COMPANY NAME, CITY & STATE   DATE
JOB TITLE
- An accomplishment from this job, illustrating a skill needed in the new job
- An accomplishment from this job, illustrating a skill needed in the new job
- An accomplishment from this job, illustrating a skill needed in the new job

OTHER EXPERIENCE
COMPANY NAME, CITY & STATE   DATE
JOB TITLE
- An accomplishment that illustrates a business skill
- An accomplishment that illustrates a business skill

ACTIVITIES
School or Community Activity   Date
School or Community Activity   Date
School or Community Activity   Date

SKILLS
Computer Skills
Foreign Languages
Writing Skills

Resumé Action Verbs

The following action verbs will help you to describe the experinces and responsibilities on your résumé clearly and concisely.

accomplished	facilitated	modified	selected
acted	generated	monitored	separated
adapted	guided	motivated	served
advised	handled	observed	simplified
aided	implemented	obtained	sold
allocated	improved	operated	solicited
analyzed	increased	organized	solved
assisted	initiated	outlined	sorted
balanced	inquired	participated	started
began	instructed	performed	studied
budgeted	insured	planned	suggested
categorized	integrated	prepared	supervised
collaborated	invented	presented	supported
compiled	involved	prioritized	surveyed
completed	joined	produced	taught
contacted	launched	programmed	tested
coordinated	learned	provided	trained
counseled	led	publicized	translated
decided	located	published	tutored
designed	made	recorded	updated
developed	maintained	reduced	used
directed	managed	reported	utilized
edited	marketed	represented	verified
established	matched	reviewed	volunteered
evaluated	measured	revised	won
expanded	met	scheduled	

Chronological Résumé

Most résumés will have five or six sections, depending on the individual's background. The chronological résumé we created for Jessica on page 34 has six sections.

   I. Name and Address
  II. Education
 III. Experience
 IV. Activities
  V. Skills
 VI. Interests

Name and Address

Everything is stacked and centered with the name in bold so that it stands out. I prefer spelling everything out because I think it looks better (e.g., Street v. St.), but it's not going to determine whether or not you get called in for an interview, so don't obsess over it.

Education

This has been your full-time career for the past four years, so don't treat it lightly. Important and impressive to include are study abroad, off-campus study, special programs, summer school, and senior research projects. Section headings are in bold caps and off to the left. The name of the institution is highlighted in bold. Again, I prefer to spell out the degree, but it's just a preference, nothing more. After you secure your first job after college, this section will move to the bottom for all subsequent résumés you create.

Experience

Margins and layout must remain consistent from one section to the next. Again, the eye is drawn to key details (i.e., where you worked) by putting the name of the company in bold. Italicizing the job title sets it apart from everything else. Bulleting the key responsibilities in concise, fragmented sentences guides the reviewer through the résumé with ease. Also, notice how the job responsibilities were expanded to demonstrate the larger scope of the experience. "General clerical" becomes "Prepared production reports; distributed news summaries."

Activities and Skills/Honors

Following the format and margins, we list Jessica's primary school and community activities after the experience section. You can get away with leaving out dates in this section because they're not as relevant as job experience. Lastly, we include information that is not job or experience related. If you are running out of space on your résumé, skills and honors can be lumped together as shown.

This is the basic format of the chronological résumé. It is concise yet descriptive, providing the essential information in an easy-to-read layout. This résumé would work for any job that Jessica was applying for. However, we can also modify the format and information very easily and tailor the résumé for a job in journalism by creating a combination résumé.

Combination Résumé

For obvious reasons, the name, address, and education sections remain the same as on the chronological résumé. However, we have eliminated the *experience* section and created a *relevant experience* section. This enables us to eliminate the two jobs that aren't related to her field and include two of her school activities that are. Grouped together under relevant experience, they present a very impressive picture. We've also moved the honors section in front of activities to highlight her journalism award. Once you have created a personal profile and use the résumé template, you can quickly and easily create a résumé on your word processor tailored to any job.

Chronological Résumé

JESSICA CUNNINGHAM
123 Main Street
Capital, USA 12345
(555) 555–1234

EDUCATION
Liberal Arts University—Rochester, MN
Bachelor of Arts Degree, May 1997
Major: History

Sorbonne—Paris, France
Spring 1996
French & European History

EXPERIENCE
ABC BROADCASTING—NEW YORK, NY   SUMMER 1996
INTERN
- Prepared production reports; distributed daily news summary
- Researched videotape and background information for feature stories and weekly news summaries
- Organized videotape library

SPARKYS RESTAURANT—OCEAN CITY, MD   SUMMER 1995
WAITRESS/BARTENDER
- Alternated managing full bar and 12-table station for busy seafood restaurant and bar

EYE ON ROCHESTER—ROCHESTER, MN   OCTOBER 1994 TO APRIL 1995
INTERN
- Collected and edited news items from the wire services
- Answered busy newsdesk telephones

OCEAN BEACH—OCEAN CITY, MD   SUMMER 1994
LIFEGUARD

ACTIVITIES
School radio and newspaper volunteer
Student government
Community recycling program volunteer

SKILLS/HONORS
- Word 6.0; Mac Photoshop; Fluent French and Italian
- Dean's List; Journalism Writing Award

Combination Résumé

JESSICA CUNNINGHAM
123 Main Street
Capital, USA 12345
(555) 555–1234

EDUCATION
Liberal Arts University—Rochester, MN
Bachelor of Arts Degree, May 1997
Major: History

Sorbonne—Paris, France
Spring 1996
French & European History

RELEVANT EXPERIENCE
ABC BROADCASTING—NEW YORK, NY   SUMMER 1996
INTERN
- Prepared production reports; distributed daily news summary
- Researched videotape and background information for feature stories and weekly news summaries
- Organized videotape library

EYE ON ROCHESTER—ROCHESTER, MN   OCTOBER 1994 TO APRIL 1995
INTERN
- Collected and edited news items from the wire services
- Answered busy newsdesk telephones

STATE UNIVERSITY NEWSPAPER—ROCHESTER, MN
COPYEDITOR

STATE UNIVEERSITY RADIO STATION—ROCHESTER, MN
NEWS REPORTER

HONORS
Excellence in Journalism Writing Award; Dean's List

ACTIVITIES
- Student government
- Community recycling program volunteer

SKILLS
Word 6.0; Mac Photoshop; Fluent French and Italian

CHAPTER FOUR

Job Search 101

Never desert your own line of talent.
Be what nature intended you for, and you will succeed.
—Sydney Smith

Career Development Office

Liberal arts students who are part of a multidiscipline university recognize the on-campus recruiting season by the parade of navy-blue-suit and white-shirt-clad business students walking seriously and self-consciously around campus like children dressed for Sunday school. Every year, graduating business students migrate to the Career Development Department, which seems to be their exclusive domain. While a few liberal arts majors may venture into this territory, most feel out of place in the midst of the investment banking, consulting, insurance, and pharmaceutical firms. The scenario isn't much different on the campuses of the small liberal arts colleges, where there aren't any business students to contend with, but there are the same limited range of firms to choose from. Liberal arts students often complain that the Career Development Department doesn't attract a broader mix of companies to recruit on campus. However, it is the nature of the each industry's recruiting process that usually dictates which firms visit your campus. Most employers do not have either the resources or the need to recruit on campus, especially firms in the more "glamorous" industries.

The companies that do send representatives to various colleges typically have training programs with a required number of positions that they must fill, usually well in advance of the training program's start date. Many of these companies need to aggressively compete with other firms with similar hiring requirements for top students in a particular discipline. They wouldn't be able to fill their training classes without on-campus recruiting. That is why some students have jobs lined up six months or more before graduation. Some firms do not have name recognition and recruit on campus to publicize their company and attract top students. Regardless of the industry you are interested in, or whether you attend a large university or small liberal arts college, the Career Development Department is still one of the most effective places to begin your job search.

While you should register with this department early in your academic career, all of the services and programs are usually still available to graduates. Developing a relationship with the career department can give you a competitive edge in your job search and provide you with a career-long resource.

Besides coordinating on-campus recruiting, the office offers a wealth of current employer information both in print and online, which can reduce your research time significantly. Also, the career office is usually the first point of contact for the many companies that do not recruit on campus but are still interested in hiring that college's students. These companies usually post job listings with the office, and your relationship with a counselor may give you the inside track. Throughout my career in human resources, I have always been willing to interview any individual who came recommended or was introduced to me by a career development office counselor with whom I've worked. Through their contacts, counselors may also be able to connect you to your target employer even if that company has never recruited or listed any positions with your school.

Many career development staffs, in cooperation with other schools, connect their students with a variety of other organizations through jointly administered off-site recruiting consortia.

Technology has also made it easier to bring a more diverse

mix of employers to students. Recently, twenty-five liberal arts colleges created the **Liberal Arts Career NetWORK,** a consortium that provides employers access to a combined pool of 60,000 liberal arts students via the Internet. Employers can have a direct link to these students by accessing their résumés, or posting jobs on one bulletin board that is shared only by the students from the participating schools. Ask if your school participates in this program.

Many departments also arrange other programs like "Career Nights," which focus on different fields, and "Job Search Seminars," where working professionals participate in panel discussions. Some departments coordinate off-site career seminars, where companies host students for a half day. Others have established "Shadowing" or "Mentor" programs, usually with alums, where students can spend a day or two inside a company and observe the day-to-day activities. In addition to learning inside information about what it is like to work in various industries, these programs also provide many potential networking contacts. Professionals who take the time to participate in these programs, whether on or off campus, will usually take the time to provide you with an informational interview, if you ask.

Another important and often underutilized service the Career Development Department can provide is a mock interview. Anyone who has never been on an interview, or who feels that they have not been interviewing successfully, should take advantage of the opportunity to practice. The career counselors are trained to critique your interviewing skills. I strongly recommend videotaping the session to identify and help you understand your strengths and weaknesses. You do not need a studio or expensive equipment—a simple camcorder will do. You may be amazed at what you will discover about how you present yourself both verbally and nonverbally. Ask yourself, Would you hire *that* person?

Perhaps the most valuable service the Career Development Office can provide is one-on-one professional guidance and support—someone to bounce ideas off, point you in the right direction, provide objective advice about what you may be doing wrong in your search, and, most important, confirm what you are doing right. Too often, job seekers lose confidence in their approach and resort to gimmicks because they have unrealistic expectations about how quickly or easily they should achieve "success," that is, a job offer. A focused job search requires hard work, diligence, confidence, and patience.

Circumstances beyond your control may influence whether your search will take weeks or months. Since these are uncharted waters for most recent graduates, a career counselor can help you stay the course and not lose confidence with a sound strategy that *will* be successful. Many job seekers pay thousands of dollars to private employment counselors and agencies for this kind of service. You have already paid much more than that in tuition. Get your money's worth.

Targeting Specific Employers

Many recent graduates make the mistake of limiting their search to the largest firms with the most name recognition in their field. However, there are thousands of small, growing companies that fuel the economy, create the most jobs, and offer exciting career opportunities that you may have never heard of. If you expand your search, you will discover more opportunities and encounter less competition, which obviously is a formula for a more efficient and successful job search.

There are many traditional directories available in most libraries that list employers by size, industry, and location. A few examples are:

- *Standard and Poor's Register of Corporations*
- *Dun & Bradstreet's Million Dollar Directory*
- *The National Job Bank*
- *Job Seeker's Guide to Public and Private Companies*
- *Hoover's Guide to Employers*

While these directories will give you listings of basic company information, other sources can provide you with more detailed information that you can use to target specific companies. Many business periodicals such as *Fortune* magazine conduct annual surveys which rate companies in various categories such as financial soundness, quality of management, quality of products and services, and, most important, ability to attract, develop, and keep talented people. *Fortune* also publishes a survey of how companies rank in their own industry. Other publications with special issues that you should review are:

- Business Weeks*'s 100 Best Small Companies*
- Fortune*'s 100 Fastest Growing Companies*
- Forbe*'s 200 Best Small Companies*
- Inc*'s 100 Fastest Growing Public Companies*
- Inc*'s 500 Most Rapidly Growing Private Companies*

Inter*Knot*—Untangling the World Wide Web

You'd have to live in a monastery to not know how important the Internet has become, but even then you'd probably have your own Web site. Web addresses appear in virtually every print publication, at the bottom of every advertisement, the back of every consumer product, and at the end of every television show and movie. A recent study by the Global Internet Project found that the World Wide Web is growing by 300,000 pages every week! The technological revolution is changing everything it touches, and the employment market is no exception. Because college students are some of the most wired-in people in the country, nearly all of the major career sites have areas devoted to college students and recent graduates.

However, if you thought the glut of career guides available in the bookstores and libraries was dizzying, the Internet—with thousands of career-related Web sites and employer "home pages"—is a cornucopia of career information that can short-circuit your brain and your job search unless you know how to sort it all out and put it in perspective. There are basically five roles the Internet can play in your job search. Let's examine the merits of each.

Career Counseling

Thousands of different sites are dedicated to offering advice on every aspect of the job search. The technology may be new, but the information is not. There is nothing new to learn on-line about how to prepare your résumé, answer interview questions, dress, etc. The Internet just provides you with access to more of the same. Don't waste your time. You know what they say about too many cooks in the kitchen . . . Simplify. Remember, there is no new, secret formula for job-search success. It is all basic, and we are handling everything you need to know right here.

Job Listings

Most recent graduates take the path of least resistance when looking for a job. They limit their efforts to responding to scores of help wanted ads or mass-mailing hundreds of unsolicited résumés, then passively waiting for a response. Well, the Internet offers a "superhighway" of least resistance with tens of thousands of job listings just a click away. However, while the path of least resistance is the most well-worn, it is also the least successful route to finding a job. That's because job listings, while the most popular method recent graduates use for finding jobs, is the least popular method employers use for filling vacancies. It is time-consuming and labor intensive for employers to fill vacancies in this manner. Employers have to write and post the job descriptions; wait for, then review, hundreds of responses; schedule appointments; and conduct a series of interviews before making an offer to someone who, at the end of this process, is still an unknown commodity. Employers would much prefer to hire someone referred to them or whom they have some firsthand knowledge of through temp, part-time, or internship work. Moreover, job listings on the Internet are not consolidated in one central site.

You would have to search through thousands of sites to find all of the listings on the Web. Even if you did have the time to hunt through every job listing on every site, it is unlikely you would find a job you'd be interested in. While many entry-level jobs are listed in the on-line data bases, the overwhelming majority aren't. And if you did find an interesting job listing, you would be competing with everyone else on the Web who accessed that listing as well as the other applicants who have the inside track through the preferred methods of recruiting we just discussed.

However, do not abandon this method entirely; just don't rely on it as your primary means for finding a job. Focus your search by targeting the companies that interest you. Review their home pages for vacancies they may list. Spend only a fraction of your time scanning the job-listing Web sites, and confine yourself to the handful of large, well-known sites like JobTrak, Monster Board, and CareerMosaic.

There are periodicals that rate Web sites, such as *WebWeek, ComputerUser, Yahoo!, Internet Life,* and *The Web.* They change as quickly as the technology, so you have to stay current.

If you are searching for a job in another city, the Internet is an invaluable resource. Many of the resources endemic to that location can be accessed from your home, including the help wanted ads from the local newspapers.

Résumé Posting

Many recent graduates post their résumés on the various on-line résumé data bases for employers to see. However, it is more likely that some cyberspace nut, not an employer, is going to access your résumé and use all of that information. Didn't you see *The Net* with Sandra Bullock? Hackers wiped out her entire existence. OK, maybe that's a little alarmist, but why take unnecessary chances?

Now that you understand the job-search process from the employer's perspective, how likely do you think it is that employers in your chosen field will come looking for you? It's just not how it works. Save yourself the time and the potential trouble.

InterNetworking

Despite the fact that the Internet is the world's largest network, it is not the most effective means to network. Through mailing lists, bulletin boards, newsgroups, and chatgroups, you may be able to make some contacts that will help you in your job search. However, the most effective networking contacts are much closer to home: family, friends, friends of friends, alumni, professors, former and current employers, and work associates. We'll discuss effective networking techniques in the next section.

Research

The real value of the Internet as part of the job-search process is its ability to provide you with current information about almost every company and industry you might be interested in. As we have discussed, the best candidates are the best prepared. They walk into the interview knowing all of the important, current information about the industry, the company, and the job. The Internet is the most exhaustive research tool in the world you can use to help you prepare, especially if you live in an area with only limited resources. You can easily access trade associations, journals, and current articles in local newspapers and news-weeklies at any time. Read the company's home page to find out what is new and important. Visit the large information data bases with employer profiles and look for links to information in your chosen field or industry. However, if you don't have access to the Internet, don't panic. Most of the resources you need to conduct your research are available in the library.

Networking—The Power to Communicate

Networking is a favorite job-search buzzword, but what does it really mean and how do you incorporate it into your job search? Unlike the complex network of technology that is the Internet, networking is simply the art of meeting people and making conversation. As a liberal arts graduate, the breadth of your studies has prepared you not only with broad knowledge but also with the critical interpersonal skills you need to enlist the help of others in your search for a job. While technology has in many ways revolutionized communication, technology cannot replace the power of basic, interpersonal human interaction—unfiltered by electrons—where all the senses are involved and required for effectively connecting with another individual.

The power to communicate will help you land the job you want and penetrate those especially hard to crack "it's who you know" industries. Do not rely on technology in the job-search process. Rely on your strengths. Pick up the phone, write a letter, meet people—communicate.

What Do You Know?

Before you approach any potential networking contact, you must first do your homework. Research the position, the company, or at the very least the industry you are interested in. Know something about your contact and his or her organization. Assume that everyone is busy and doesn't want to spend time helping you find yourself or answering basic questions you should have researched beforehand.

What Do You Want—Really?

What you are asking for is an informational interview. You want that person's insider insight and advice. Informational interviews help you discover hidden pathways to particular jobs. Although your goal is a job, never ask for one when networking. Potential contacts are more likely to meet with you if you ask for their help and advice. Asking for a job puts people on the spot and makes them uncomfortable.

Everyone knows you are looking for a job. The informational interview is really a job interview in disguise, but without the added pressure and expectations. Approach the interview with the same degree of preparation and professionalism as you would a regular job interview. Bring a résumé, but don't offer it unless it is requested. If the meeting goes well and they do know of an available position, they will tell you about it, or hopefully will think of you when a position does become available. At the end of the meeting, ask if they know of anyone else they can refer you to for assistance, but (it is worth repeating because it happens frequently) do not ask if they have any openings. It is a betrayal of the unspoken condition upon which they agreed to meet with you in the first place—a safe, informational meeting where they won't be put on the spot.

Who Do You Know? Expanding Your Universe

They say there are only six degrees of separation between any two people in the world. This is where the path of least resistance is your best strategy because it offers the greatest opportunity for success. Start close to home with family and friends.

While they may be a few steps away from the person you actually need to speak to, it's safe to practice your networking technique on them, and they in turn may have a vested interest in helping you, like getting you out of the house and off their "payroll." Branch out in the family tree. Even if you should have been nicer to weird Uncle Al all of these years, if he works in your chosen profession, or knows someone who does, hit him up for help. Look for opportunities to expand your circle of contacts—not just friends, but friends and family of friends, and so on. Don't forget current and former employers and work associates, professors (especially those who come out of the business environment), and other school contacts. Two of the most efficient networking sources are college alumni and trade associations because they may lead directly to the contacts who can hire you. Alumni networks are a powerful networking resource because they exist primarily for networking purposes. Alums feel almost obligated to meet with fellow alums seeking advice. Finally, trade associations may be the most direct link to the people who can help you. Rarely do recent graduates make use of this rich resource. Almost every field has an association of professionals working in that industry. Check out the *Encyclopedia of Associations* published by Gale Research. It includes a list of over 25,000 associations. Many have local chapters and offer student memberships at reduced rates. Join the association for your chosen profession and obtain a membership directory, which includes every member's name, address, telephone number, title, and company.

If you continue to network after you get your first job, you may never have to search for a job again. Expand your circle of personal and professional contacts by being active in trade associations, professional and social events. If you are talented and work to stay visible, enough people in the right places will notice and opportunities may continue to present themselves to you throughout your career.

Making Contact

> *"Hello, may I speak with Janice, please." "She's sleeping. Can you call back?" "This is Mr. Peterson from XYZ Corporation returning her call." "Oh, hold on a minute."* (Heard in the background) *"J? J? Jan? Wake up! It's some guy from some company on the phone. I don't know who, Peter something."*

The telephone is the most effective networking tool for initiating contact. Unfortunately, many recent graduates do not know how to use the telephone effectively. Here's a primer on telephone technique and etiquette:

- Try to reach your contact directly by calling during off-peak hours. Before 9 A.M. and after 5 P.M. is usually best.
- Long-winded introductions and voice-mail messages make people nuts. Whether you reach the individual directly or get their voice mail, state who you are, how you got their name, and what you want in fifteen seconds or less.
- If you fail to reach the individual or voice mail, be courteous to whomever answers the phone, and if the assistant doesn't put you through, remember, they are only doing their job.
- The receptionist or assistant does not have the time to take complicated messages. Keep it simple.
- Get an answering machine.
- Change those sophomoric answering machine messages: "Hey, you've reached Ben and Jerry. No, not the ice-cream makers, dude—anyway, we're out partying . . ."
- Be professional when answering the phone at home—no loud music blaring in the background.
- Alert your family or roommate that you are expecting a call and remind them to answer the call waiting.
- Have your notes and a pen nearby so that you do not have to fumble for them during the call.

If these pointers seem obvious to you, congratulations—you are ahead of your competition.

Cover Letters

Everyone loves to get mail. One of the first things most people do when they come home is check the mail. Typically, we shuffle through bills and all of the junk mail labeled RESIDENT, pause momentarily at the clever marketing pieces that seem personalized but are really mass mailings, and finally pay close attention to the letters truly addressed to us. The ritual is the same at work. When applying for a job, every letter addressed "To Whom It May Concern" is met with the same reaction as RESIDENT. A personalized cover letter can be one of your most effective tools for distinguishing yourself from the bulk mail. This is where your research and networking efforts can pay dividends. Get a name. Demonstrate that you are not just looking for a job by doing an impersonal mass mailing to organizations selected blindly from a directory. Rather, you have chosen them specifically because you know who they are, what they do, and how well they do it. Emphasize what you can contribute to their organization in particular.

Write it in your own words so that it sounds like you, not something you copied out of a cover letter book. The tone of the letter and the knowledge, enthusiasm, and focus that you demonstrate add dimension and texture to the content of the résumé that will help set it and you apart from the crowd.

Whether you are applying for a job or soliciting advice from a networking contact, the basic format of the letter is the same. I have modified the following Cover Letter Templates from a version the Career Development Office at Denison University distributes to their students, which expertly summarizes the anatomy of the cover letter and how to use it successfully.

JOB SEARCH COVER LETTER TEMPLATE

Current Address
City, State, Zip Code

Month & Day, Year

Name of Person to Whom You Are Writing
Title
Name of Organization
Street Address
City, State, Zip Code

Dear (Mr./Ms.) Last Name:

State why you are writing. Indicate the position about which you are writing and tell them how you became aware of the position as appropriate.

Refer the reader to the enclosed résumé. Mention one or two main qualifications that you think would be of greatest interest to the employer, tailoring your remarks to them. If you have related experience or specialized training, be sure to point it out. However, do not repeat your entire résumé. Indicate why you are particularly interested in their organization or type of work.

Restate your interest and availability for an interview. Indicate that you will be contacting them within a given length of time in the hopes of scheduling an interview. Thank them for their time and consideration.

Sincerely,

(Your Handwritten Signature)

Your Typed Name

Enclosure

NETWORKING COVER LETTER TEMPLATE

Current Address
City, State, Zip Code

Month & Day, Year

Name of Person to Whom You Are Writing
Title
Name of Organization
Street Address
City, State, Zip Code

Dear (Mr./Ms.) Last Name:

Mention the referral source—be it another person, trade association, alumni office, or article in which the networking contact was quoted. State why you are writing to them
specifically—flattery will get you everywhere!

Include some personal information about yourself—the
school you have or will be graduating from, your career
plans, one or two main qualifications, etc. State that you are
gathering information about a particular career. Politely in-
quire about the possibility of an informational interview.

Restate your interest in the field. Indicate that you will be
contacting them within a given length of time about the possibility of scheduling a meeting at their convenience. Provide
a telephone number where you can be reached in the meantime. Thank them for their time and consideration.

Sincerely,

(Your Handwritten Signature)

Your Typed Name

CHAPTER FIVE

Advanced Job Search

It is a mistake to look too far ahead.
Only one link in the chain of destiny can be handled at a time.

—Sir Winston Churchill

W The Best-Kept Secret Method for Conducting Your Job Search

hat if I told you that you that beginning today, immediately, you could get paid to conduct your job search? Paid as much as the equivalent of $30,000 per year. And while you were getting paid, you could get the inside track on many positions; upgrade your computer skills and learn any new software program for free; walk right into almost any company and research it firsthand; and gain valuable job skills, industry knowledge, and contacts. In the process, you would eliminate the need to scour the want ads or job postings; write cover letters; mail out dozens of résumés; make dozens of phone calls; and wait home anxiously for the phone to ring. Sound too good to be true? Well, it's not. You can do it easily and immediately, and it is just as effective for those who know what they want to do as for those who don't. It's called *temping*. And liberal arts majors are prepared for the challenges posed by temping. The breadth of your experiences and studies makes you uniquely qualified to succeed in a variety of settings and environments. And the scope of the assignments and responsibilities you receive would not be very different from what you would probably be doing anyway in many industries in an entry-level position.

Gone are the days when a stigma was attached to temporary employment. Today, the temporary worker is an invaluable resource increasingly relied upon as companies respond to a competitive marketplace by "reengineering" to become more productive and cost-effective. Large blue-chip behemoths like IBM and AT&T, former bastions of job security, have eliminated staff positions. Smaller, growing companies are reluctant to add to their staffs too quickly and increase overhead. Instead, corporations have been utilizing the services of millions of temporary employees without incurring the costs associated with filling traditional jobs, such as the recruiting expense and time, not to mention benefits.

Today, 95 percent of all companies employ temps to supplement their full-time staffs. Temps were once just fill-in secretaries and file clerks; today they are representative of all educational and skill levels. Sixty-two percent of temporary workers have at least some college education. Twenty percent of temporary workers temp as a way to look for their first full-time job.

Temporary workers fill in for absent employees or for special projects where an "extra pair of hands" is needed for a short period of time. Truly outstanding temps get noticed. Often a company will say of a terrific temporary worker, "The temp I have is great. Is she looking for a job?" Nearly 40 percent of all temporary workers are offered full-time jobs at the company to which they are assigned.

Temping is also convenient if you don't interview well. You can step right into a job and knock their socks off without the interview. You get to try a position, boss, and company on for size with no obligation. And the company does the same with you. There is less of an unknown with hiring temps, because the company gets to see their work and how they interact with others, which is very appealing to employers. Temping can also be a much less stressful way to start your first job.

How to Temp Search

Searching for a job through temping requires a great deal of flexibility and diligence. You must be a self-starter and quick learner, and have the ability to adapt to changing dynamics and expectations. You must also be reliable. The following list will help you get started:

1. Most temporary agencies advertise in the help-wanted section of the local newspaper. Check the Sunday section, where you are likely to find every agency in your area.
2. Check the yellow pages. Most large firms will be listed.
3. Ask everyone you know who has a job to find out which temporary agency their company uses. Get the name and telephone number of the representative who services the account.
4. Call companies you are interested in working for and ask which temporary agency they use. Try the human resources department, since they probably coordinate the temporary employees. You can also try and call any other department. Just tell the person on the other end of the phone honestly that you are interested in working for that company but would like to get a feel for the place by temping. It will work every time. Someone will tell you which service they use. You may even speak to a temp.

Signing Up With an Agency

1. Make appointments with several agencies.
2. Treat the appointment as you would any interview: Arrive on time, appropriately dressed, with a copy of your résumé.
3. You will be required to fill out several forms and take a series of tests including typing, whatever word-processing software you are familiar with, spelling, grammar, and math.
4. You will then have an interview with a counselor. This interview is very important because agencies have their A-list of proven temps, and at this point you are an unknown. You will want to establish a good relationship with your counselor. Ask them which industries they place temporary workers in, and tell them what you're interested in.

You should register with as many agencies as you can until one of them begins offering you assignments in interesting companies. Once you click with one agency, stick with them. If you work well together, it is a mutually beneficial relationship and they will want to keep you happy.

From the Agency Side

Temporary agencies are in a very competitive business and their livelihoods, and reputations, depend on the quality of the service, and the temps, they provide, and the relationships they forge. Agencies enter into an agreement with a company to provide them with temporary workers, usually on short notice. The quality of an agency is measured in several ways. Many of the fundamental traits are the same that most companies look for in the people they hire as staff. They are *dependability, productivity,* and *interpersonal skills.*

Depending on the assignment, a company may need anything from a warm body to stuff envelopes to a polished and highly skilled assistant for the CEO. If a temporary worker does not fulfill the assignment satisfactorily, shows up late, makes lots of personal phone calls, or isn't conscientious because he or she is "just a temp," it is a reflection on the temp agency's ability to screen and refer quality workers. The temp agency likely will not offer you any more assignments.

For example, there was a highly polished executive secretary who worked wonderfully for the CEO of a major corporation for two months while the regular assistant was on maternity leave. When the warm weather came around, the temp began sunbathing during her lunch hours in a thong bikini in front of the building! That certainly is one way to get off the agency's A-list!

Your First Assignment

When you do get an assignment, make the agency look good, and they will quickly move you to the A-list for the plum, higher-paying assignments. The agency will put you on their payroll and agree to pay you a certain rate for each assignment they send you on. The agency bills the company at a markup to cover their costs, and, of course, earn a profit. Everyone gets something. You will chart your hours worked each day and have the supervisor at the company sign off on the sheet you submit to the agency. They will pay you weekly and have your normal taxes deducted as any employee would. After you have successfully completed a number of assignments or hours, they will usually give you the opportunity to learn advanced word-processing systems for free, so they will have even more assignments they can send you out on, for more money.

Commitment

Temping also gives you with the flexibility to have some fun. There's nothing like going to the beach on a Tuesday morning or the Wednesday matinee when everyone else is working. However, if you agree to a one-week assignment, then they are depending on you to work that entire week. Keep that commitment. If you are conducting a concurrent job search and you have interviews, schedule them on lunch hours, before or after work, or on a day when you haven't committed to temping. Don't worry about losing the opportunity to interview because of your schedule. Any company interested in you will try to be accommodating, within reason. Your unwillingness to compromise the commitment you made to your temp employer and agency will reflect positively on your character and work ethic, which any company you may interview with would have to admire.

On the Job

Arrive early and dressed professionally. Take this work as seriously as you do a regular job. Think of each assignment as an audition. Remember, many a star was born from very small roles, so even if you are asked to file, perform like no one has ever filed before.

Demonstrate a positive attitude and, most important, initiative. Your ability to figure things out, get the lay of the land on your own, and contribute quickly will get you recognized.

During your lunch hour, make sure to note names and phone numbers of key department heads and human resources staff so that you can contact them directly after the assignment ends. This is valuable information that would either be impossible to get otherwise or would take hours of research and telephone calls to obtain. Look at company job postings and in-house newsletters for more information. Obtain copies of company literature and annual reports; again, this is information that you have at your fingertips that would be difficult to get otherwise. It's like being a kid in a candy store, so take advantage of it.

Sometimes companies order temps for assignments that require very little work. Don't be content to just sit there and answer phones. Employers frequently don't expect much initiative from temps, so there can be a tendency to relax. Don't. Tell them that you are capable of doing a lot more, and that you are not being utilized to your fullest potential. Try to identify areas where you can help. They may not want to take the time to teach you how to do more because you are a temp. Don't just ask to do more—take it upon yourself to do more. Volunteer to stay late; don't just walk out the door at 5 P.M. Treat the job and the experience as if it were your career. If you do not like the assignment, ask the agency to reassign you. Never just leave or refuse to return unless you are put in an abusive situation. Give the agency time to reassign you and refill the position.

Network

In a record book log every assignment, company name, address, contacts, telephone numbers, and dates. Develop a rapport with other people you work with; log their information as well. Collect as many business cards as you can. Before the assignment ends, make sure to network. Ask to speak to your boss, other department heads, anyone you'd like to meet for a few minutes. Tell them what you are looking for, ask if they know anyone that you can talk to. Don't waste their time: be specific. Don't rely on other people to figure out what you want to do. If you are interested in working for that organization, then treat it like an interview. Leave them a copy of your résumé and make certain to meet with human resources personnel if you can. Follow-up with thank-you notes for the experience.

Infiltrate the Headquarters

Ask for temp assignments in a human resources departments—the center of all hiring activity. There is rarely a more powerful ally in the company. And, since the human resources department is usually the one that orders the temps, you might get the inside track on other plum temp assignments right from the company itself. It's likely they will call the agency and ask them to put you on the company's A-list.

Temping also enables you to build your résumé by upgrading computer and job skills. It also takes off some of the pressure to make money, which is the most common reason recent grads take first jobs they aren't really interested in. Don't worry what temping looks like on your résumé. It's better than not working. *Tempsearching* can be very impressive to an employer.

Getting yourself involved in the day-to-day routine of the working world, meeting people, and successfully adapting to the challenges posed by temping is something you can play up when going on job interviews. While everyone else is pounding on employer's doors trying to get in for an interview, you waltzed right in with an invitation. That's impressive.

CHAPTER SIX

The Interview

Sometimes I lie awake at night, and I ask, where have I gone wrong? Then a voice says to me, this is going to take more than one night.

—"Charlie Brown"

The Big Date

Maybe you respond to an ad that seems to be a perfect match. Perhaps a mutual acquaintance sets you up. You probably trade phone calls before finally speaking to each other. You acknowledge that you've heard a lot about each other, and eventually decide to make a date.

You hate blind dates. Your expectations have always been high because you're an optimist, but you can't help feeling a little jaded. You've been through this several times before, only to be disappointed because it hasn't worked out. Sure, once or twice you thought there was something there, but it just never panned out.

But you acknowledge that this is just how the game is played, and you never now when you will finally click with someone, so you begin to prepare. What should you wear? What should you say? Just be yourself, you're not desperate, you remind yourself.

Finally the big day comes, and as usual you're running late, but somehow, as always, you manage to pull it all together and get there on time, looking your best. You sit waiting, wondering if each passerby might be the one. You've only spoken on the phone, but the mind can draw vivid pictures.

You recognize that pang in your stomach, the combination of exhilaration, nerves, and expectations as the two of you finally meet, with plastered smiles and outstretched hands. You exchange a few pleasantries you won't recall five minutes later, and finally settle down into conversation. Your senses are on alert as you simultaneously send and receive verbal and nonverbal signals, hoping to penetrate the veneer of courtesy. Time seems to be suspended until you are reminded by subtle verbal clues and shifts in body language that the parting pleasantries are about to end. The end of the first encounter is always as awkward as the beginning.

You say good-bye, usually already knowing whether or not either of you is interested in meeting again. You search for some lighthearted comment to ease the strain of the moment, feeling awkwardly self-conscious as you depart.

It's worse if you're interested but aren't sure if they are. You sit home waiting, wondering when and if they will call, rehashing every insignificant detail and pretending not to care, preparing yourself for disappointment. Should you call first? You decide not to. You relish the moment you get the call you've been hoping for—the feeling of being wanted—and the courtship begins.

It's Not Science

You've done this before; how successfully I don't know, but more than likely you've been through the interview ritual many times, even if you've never applied for a job. A first date, a chance meeting at a party, or a setup by a mutual acquaintance. Depending upon how successful those encounters have been, you're either panicking or are comforted by the knowledge that you have already done this successfully. The interview process, especially for entry-level positions, has been so blown out of proportion that one book on the subject outrageously suggests keeping a resin bag like baseball pitchers use in your trousers to ward against sweaty palms! If you weren't nervous about interviewing before, you certainly might be after reading that. That is not to say that interviewing isn't uncomfortable, because it can be. Let's face it, everything is riding on the interview. It is how employers determine whether or not you are a general fit with the organization and whether or not you will get the job.

However, your liberal arts studies have prepared you for the interview. And once you understand the interview from the employer's side of the desk—what criteria they use, how and why they make their decisions—your interview will be less anxious, more successful, and even, I hope, enjoyable.

Remember all of the work that went into crafting your résumé? When it comes right down to it, it is not going to get you the job over the other applicants. Most recent graduates fail to grasp this fundamental point, leaving them unprepared for the interview.

While most interviews revolve around the information that is contained in your résumé, that information is not the key element. Actually, once you've secured the interview, it frequently doesn't even matter. What is most important, what employers look for, and what will ultimately get you the job over the other candidates is the attitude, presence, and intelligence you display during the interview.

It is common for applicants, when asked to describe their experience or activities, to respond, "Well, it's right there on the résumé. What more do you want to know?" At this point the interviewer thinks to himself, "What I want to know is how quickly I can get you out of my office." Obtaining an entry-level job is not about what is on your résumé. It is about articulating who you are, what you've done, and what you want. It is about demonstrating an understanding of the industry and job you are applying for. Furthermore, it is about articulating your knowledge of the employer and why you want to work for that company in particular. Ultimately, it comes down to something as simple as whether they like you or not. Considering most people spend more time with their co-workers than their loved ones, an employer is looking for someone they would like having around, someone who will make a positive contribution not just professionally but to the environment of the company. Is there chemistry? Do you fit? Does it seem right? Just like dating. Many people get turned down for jobs for reasons that never show up in rejection letters such as appearance, lack of enthusiasm, poor verbal skills, and attitude.

Another common mistake is approaching an interview as if it were a one-sided meeting, hoping the employer will choose you over everyone else. Applicants feel that because jobs are the hot commodity, the employer holds all of the cards. Wrong. You hold some cards of your own.

The interview is a two-way street. Intelligent, hardworking, mature, enthusiastic individuals with positive attitudes are the truly hot commodity. Applicants who hold those cards and play them properly are very successful in their job search. Remember, the interview is just as much about you interviewing the company to see if it is a place you want to be. The interview is about making that match, and applicants who know their value will be more desired by employers.

Employer Research

Before your interview, you must prepare by doing some homework. One of the biggest mistakes applicants make is not preparing for the interview by researching the company and the industry. There are numerous sources you can turn to for information about any company in any industry, so there is no excuse for not knowing the most basic information about the company, such as:

1. Primary products/services
2. History and growth
3. Position in industry/current market
4. Projections for future
5. Competitors
6. Size in terms of employees and revenues, and relation to competition
7. Career paths within the organization

An applicant who walks into Apple Computers not knowing that, in response to a continuing trend of losing market share to IBM, Apple laid off 3,000 workers in 1997; or that AT&T recently laid off 10,000 employees; or that Boeing acquired

McDonnel Douglas and is now the world's largest maker of jet-liners, is unprepared for the interview with those companies and will probably not get the job. Only by researching a company can you properly engage in a meaningful dialogue about why you want to work in that industry and for their company in particular.

Each company that you interview with should feel that you want a job with *them*. Your ability to make a company feel that way will give you a tremendous edge. Treat the employer as if their company is special, and they will treat you as if you are special. Treat them as if they are one of a dozen of companies, and they will treat you as if you are just one of a dozen applicants. However, insincerity is transparent, so don't try to fake it.

A Few Words About Dress

If you've gotten this far, then I feel we are close enough for me to be direct: "What's the deal with the body-piercing?" More and more students walk into my classroom with their flesh pierced in places I didn't know could be pierced. I am not stereotyping here—not all students have a penchant for puncturing themselves—but it does appear that this is one area where the business students have it all over liberal arts students. You just don't see many business majors walking around with studs in their tongues and safety pins in their eyebrows. Do you actually wake up one day and say, "Hey, I'm bored, why don't I go and stick a pin through my bellybutton today after class?"

Fortunately, most have the good sense to remove said objects before they begin the job search, but not all. My colleagues and I have come across several misguided souls who have shown up on interviews with their lips, nostrils, or eyebrows adorned with various jewelry. If it didn't occur to you that it might be inappropriate for an interview, and it is, that tells me something about your judgment. If body-piercing is common for the company or industry in which you are applying, then by all means, self-mutilate; but if you're not sure, it's usually best to play it safe. Even employers in the most relaxed business environments expect interviewees to dress conservatively for the interview.

These can be sensitive topics, but I have to tell it to you straight. Body-piercing is not the most common mistake applicants make. Hair, makeup, clothes, and other jewelry are also important. The interview is not a beauty contest, but our appearance says a lot about who we are and how we want to be perceived. The saying goes, "You never get a second chance to make a first impression." It is human nature to form instant opinions based on appearance, and interviewers aren't exempt.

You may have been less concerned about your appearance in college than you need to be now that you have graduated. Even if you worked while in college, employers make certain allowances for students. But once you graduate, rules and expectations change. Looking like or being perceived as a "student" will hurt you in your job search. You want to make an impression that suggests professionalism and maturity. Invest in your personal grooming. Get a good haircut, not one that looks like you used one of those home haircut vacuum products. It is fine to have your ears pierced, but one piece of jewelry in each ear is sufficient. Buy a few different interview outfits. You will probably have more than one interview with a company, and you don't want to repeat an outfit. Keep the outfits simple and basic. You don't have to wear designer clothes, but take a cue from most upscale designers. The clothes are classic and timeless, with clean lines and subtle colors and patterns. Nothing loud, cheap-looking, or ill-fitting. Pay attention to the small details; people notice nicely shined shoes, clean fingernails, pressed shirts. It shouldn't look as though you put too much thought or effort into dressing. You should look comfortable in your clothes, like you've worn them before, not like a child dressed for Sunday school tugging at his collar.

Business students tend to stick to a uniform: navy blue suits, white shirts or blouses; it's hard to screw that up. However, liberal arts majors, not bound by the same convention, seem to take more chances. Once you have the job, then you can follow the common dress observed by the employees. Seems obvious, but if this weren't an issue, I wouldn't have mentioned it.

Pack the Night Before

The last thing you need to worry about is whether not you have everything you need. Pack light. You don't want to fumble with bags. Besides the normal items you carry in your wallet or purse, you should also carry a briefcase with several clean copies of your résumé, your reference list, a notepad and pen, and a magazine to read (newsprint can smudge on your hand). However, make sure you read the newspaper the day of the interview. It would be embarrassing if your company made the news that day with an announcement of a big merger or acquisition and you weren't aware of it. Resist the temptation to bring research information about the company. If you don't know it by now, forget it. You will probably only make yourself more nervous by trying to cram.

The Interview

It begins the moment you walk out of the door on your way to the company. Make sure you know where you are going and how to get there. You should leave yourself plenty of time so that you don't make the cardinal sin of showing up late. If you are traveling to the interview by public transportation, be on your best interview behavior. You don't know who you may be sitting next to, arguing over a seat with, flirting with, or scratching yourself in front of.

Once while riding the bus to work, I couldn't help overhearing a job-search conversation. Two friends were on their way to interviews for jobs that neither seemed particularly interested in. They talked about how they hated interviewing with personnel departments because it was such a waste of time. Unfortunately for one of them, his interview was with my department. I walked into the building right behind him, and we rode up the elevator together—I could barely contain myself. I never told him, but I did inform my colleague, who took special delight in conducting a particularly grueling interview.

It is worth repeating: do not arrive late. Arriving late is only acceptable if you're in an accident or the victim of some sort of natural disaster, which in most cases would require that the interview be canceled anyway. It makes a terrible first impression that is difficult to overcome. Many interviewers have a fifteen-minute rule, meaning that they won't even conduct the interview if the person is more than fifteen minutes late. Arriving too early, although not nearly as egregious as being late, can be awkward because you will probably just increase your wait in the reception area. Showing up no more than ten to fifteen minutes prior to the scheduled time is appropriate. Plan to get to your interview thirty minutes early to allow for unforseen delays. You can always kill time in a nearby coffee shop or take a quick walk around the block until it is time. The last thing you want to do is increase your stress by racing to the interview.

Whenever you finally do arrive, go to the restroom. If you've ever come home from a date, looked in the mirror and noticed a piece of spinach stuck in your teeth from dinner, you'll understand why this is necessary. Check yourself out; take one last look to make sure nothing came loose during the commute and everything is where it is supposed to be. We've all had our share of applicants whose hair had been blown up from the wind like Buckwheat, with lipstick on their teeth, their zippers undone, jacket collars turned up, or foreign objects dangling from their nose. It is distracting, and not what you want the interviewer to be thinking about.

Receptionist

I haven't figured out why so many books describe the receptionist in a sexist, condescending manner. Often described as "Helga from the Gulag" or "Greta the Guardian of the Gate," the receptionist is usually a pleasant individual; that is why they are receptionists. This is an important person who has more influence than you think. The person conducting the interview will frequently ask the receptionist for their first impression of candidates. Other times the receptionist will just volunteer an opinion, especially if there is something particularly outstanding, positive or negative, about the applicant. It pays to make a special effort to be polite and strike up conversation with the receptionist if you can do so naturally and without disrupting their job.

Make certain to follow their directions, and if they ask you to fill out the entire application, even though your résumé carries all the same information, do it. Many employers do not want you to write "See Résumé Attached" because the application is a legal document and they may want a record of your credentials in case your résumé gets separated from the application.

Do not forget as you are sitting there that the interview is officially underway. Be conscious of your body language. Project confidence. Sit poised, erect, open, and don't forget to smile. Not like you're giddy or loopy. Just look welcoming, like a person with whom someone would want to sit down next to and talk. Too many applicants look as if they're waiting in the dentist's office for a root canal. Relax. You are prepared. This is a new time in your life. You should be excited by the prospect of meeting new people, learning something new, and possibly starting something new.

Showtime

When the time arrives, greet the interviewer with a warm smile, direct eye contact, and a firm handshake. Address the interviewer as Mr. or Ms. unless and until otherwise directed. Remember the importance of first impressions. The interviewer is consciously and subconsciously forming opinions about you and you about him, just like any two people who meet for the first time. Unless there is something way off base about your actions or appearance, it is unlikely that any final judgments will be based on this thirty-second encounter. However, you may be surprised to learn that a final judgment about your candidacy is likely to be made within the first five minutes of the interview.

Think about it. A lifetime of experiences, four years of college, a beautiful résumé, brand-new suit, and it all comes down to five minutes. The interviewer spends the remaining time of the interview generally looking for signs that confirm his initial decision. If you do not start off strong, you have an uphill battle because you will be spending the bulk of the interview trying to change the interviewer's mind. It can be done, but it is difficult.

Many human resources professionals and hiring managers are reluctant to admit this publicly. However, I've met individuals in all industries across the country who confess this truism privately. If the chemistry is right, the interview can flow smoothly like two friends discussing common interests. If not, the interview may proceed pleasantly but perfunctorily, with the outcome long since decided, and the real reason you didn't get the job will be couched in an explanation such as, "We hired another candidate whose background was more suitable to the position."

Interviewing Q & A

"Tell me something about yourself." This question strikes fear in the hearts of job applicants. Yet the interview is about demonstrating your social presence and maturity. It's about your ability to articulate your enthusiasm and sincere desire to work for that company, to engage the interviewer in conversation about a range of topics, including your knowledge about yourself and the employer's needs. The nature of liberal arts studies, the breadth and scope of issues that you have studied, has prepared you well. The problem with many of the books devoted to interviewing is that they overcomplicate the process. Most books talk about the "Interviewing Game," and how to win it by giving you the best answers to the most difficult or common interview questions. The result is applicants who are incorrectly prepared—often acting coached and rehearsed, reciting memorized "right" answers to specific questions.

Some employers share the blame by adopting an interview style that establishes an unnatural dynamic, leaving applicants feeling they are disadvantaged if they don't rehearse. However, most interviews are not strict Q & A, with someone firing questions at you as if you were a contestant on a quiz show, scoring points for every "correct" answer. They are usually conversations between two people just trying to get to know each other a little better. The most effective way to prepare for any interview is to know yourself, know the company, and understand what the employer is looking for.

Almost every interview question revolves around the why and how of your résumé: the two questions that provide the most insight into your attitude, work ethic, character, and maturity. The interview is about why and how you have made important decisions and handled certain situations. Knowing what information the employers are looking for will help you answer just about any interview question comfortably, without having to memorize and recite canned answers to hundreds of different questions.

Interview Styles and Tips

Everyone has their own interviewing style, and some interviewers are better than others. Usually human resources professionals are skilled interviewers because it is a primary function of their job. However, the interviewing abilities of hiring managers can range widely, and understanding that most employers are interested in the why and how gives you an inside edge. Here are a number of other tips to help you present yourself in the most positive light regardless of the interviewer's style and ability:

Be yourself. Most advice suggests that you be yourself on an interview. This is an oversimplification. Everyone has many "selves" that they display in different circumstances. Remember, they are hiring you, not your résumé or your major. They don't know very much about you yet, so you must present the side that matters in this situation—your emotional intelligence, social presence, maturity, positive attitude, and potential for growth and success.

Listen. Do not interrupt the interviewer or try to anticipate her questions before she is finished speaking. You will have your turn. Listen carefully to the question and respond directly to the question asked. This skill is a valuable trait both professionally and personally. Poor listening skills is a common problem for entry-level employees, who are sometimes overly eager to demonstrate how much they know. There is more that you don't know. Listening well will help you learn more, and more effectively.

Be concise. Applicants tend to ramble, not knowing when to finish talking because they fear awkward silence. If the interview style is informal, just be careful not to monopolize the conversation. The interviewer has other appointments and work to do and has probably scheduled only thirty to forty-five minutes for the meeting. They also have an agenda of areas they want to cover. If the interview is more structured, listen to the question, pause for a moment if you need to, and then construct a concise, precise answer. Avoid lengthy monologues. There is no rule, but one- to two-minute responses to most questions is usually comfortable and sufficient. When you feel you've answered the question completely, stop talking.

Some "stress" interviewers play games to see how long before an applicant becomes uncomfortable with the silence and feels compelled to continue speaking, which often results in rambling. This rarely occurs, but if the interviewer tries it, sit confidently, secure that you've answered the question fully, and wait.

Maintain direct eye contact. The inability to look the interviewer directly in the eye is distracting and implies nervousness and insincerity. Maintaining eye contact is a powerful, effective method of communication that projects confidence. However, please remember to observe the norms of social etiquette and avoid staring down your "opponent" in dominance, or unnerving him or her with a hypnotic trance-like gaze.

Be mindful of your body language. You can often say as much with your posture, facial expressions, and gestures as you do with words. Frequently, the confidence and traits that applicants demonstrate verbally are betrayed by the messages they send nonverbally. Sit openly upright, and forward in your seat—not closed up with your arms crossed, or slouched apathetically.

Be proud but humble. There is a fine line between confidence and arrogance. Most people are uncomfortable talking about themselves, feeling that it is bragging. Instead, be proud of your accomplishments and discuss them confidently. That is the purpose of the interview. If you feel a little uncomfortable doing that, then your natural humility will come through and no one will think you're arrogant. Individuals who aren't the least bit constrained by self-consciousness when touting their achievements often do come across as arrogant because they often are arrogant. Modesty is hard to fake.

Don't be trite. Most employers have interviewed thousands of applicants. Do you know how often they have heard "I'm a people person," and "I'm creative," "I like to see projects through to completion," "I'm a perfectionist"? Thousands of times. These are empty, hackneyed responses. Be specific about your strengths. Approach every question as an opportunity to discuss the experiences and activities that demonstrate your strengths.

Don't wait for them to ask. Tell them what you want them to know. Some interviewers aren't very good or even comfortable with conducting interviews. Most questions fall into two categories, open and closed. Open questions such as "Tell me something about yourself" are the best because they provide you with an opportunity to shape answers that present you in the most positive light. Poor interviewers may ask many closed questions, which require only a yes or no answer, such as "Did you like college?"

You should always turn closed questions into open answers. "Yes I did like college because . . ." Don't wait for the interviewer to ask you questions that present you with an opportunity to sell yourself; take that opportunity each time you respond.

Be positive. No one wants to work with a complainer. Always look for the positive—what you learned from each situation—without being negative. If you are asked what you didn't like about a certain experience, turn the question around and speak positively about how you benefited from the experience even if you were unhappy.

Pay attention to clues that the interview is ending. Too often applicants can't sense that the interviewer is trying to wrap things up. Don't make them shove you out of the office. The surest sign that you are approaching the end is when the interviewer offers you the opportunity to ask questions, shuffles papers, or stands up and looks at his watch.

Ask questions. Do not pass up the opportunity to ask questions. This is where your knowledge of the company, not to mention how well you listened during the interview, will be beneficial. The quality of your questions is just as important as the substance of the answers you've provided. Your questions should demonstrate an awareness of the employer's needs and how you can help meet those needs. Questions should not be about salary and benefits.

Strong close. Find out what the next step is in the interviewing process before leaving the office. How long before they expect to make a decision, how will you be notified, and when can you expect to hear from them? Ask if you can have the interviewer's business card, and thank them for their time.

Now that you know what employers are looking for and the fundamental tips for successful interviewing, you are prepared to handle any interview question or style effectively. The following is a list of the most commonly asked questions of entry-level applicants. Do *not* memorize specific answers to specific questions. The interview is not like a test where you get excited or stressed every time you try to remember the answer to a specific question—"yes, I know this one!" or "Damn, what was that again?" Rather, use the list to help you identify and approach the questions an interviewer might ask to find out whether you might make a good member of their team. All these different questions essentially boil down to that same goal. Therefore, all of your responses should be constructed with that in mind.

"Tell me something about yourself." The king of all open questions! Actually more of a command than a question. This is what *every* question is about. Where do you begin? What do you include? How far back do you go and how long do you go on for? Personal statistics (where you grew up, how many brothers and sisters you have) are irrelevant. Beginning with your education and a few examples of experiences that have prepared you for the job are good starting points for interviews that begin this broadly.

"Take me through your résumé, what you've done and why." You can only pray that an interviewer has this style, basically opening the floor for you to tell them whatever you want. Sometimes it is easier to focus when you have to answer specific quesitons. However, you have less control in that type of interview. This request, like the one above, is basically saying, "Okay, sell yourself. Tell me why I should hire you. What makes you different from everyone else?" Go for it! You know what they need and want. Give it to them. Don't rehash everything that they can read off the résumé. Elaborate on your experiences, activities, accomplishments, and how they relate to the job. Demonstrate your strengths and your knowledge of the company and the industry. If they are going to give you the floor like this, keep going until you are directed otherwise.

"What led you to choose your field of study/major?" Answer every question assertively, not, "I don't know. I couldn't decide on a major." Think about what is important about your particular field, what you learned, and how it specifically applies not only to business but life in general.

"How would you describe yourself? What are your greatest strengths? How would other people describe you? Why should I hire you?" These are all essentially the same question. It is an invitation to mention the skills and traits you possess that you know that the employer is looking for and are important for the job.

Remember, anyone can recite superlatives. Be specific and provide examples of accomplishments, situations, and experiences that demonstrate the various strengths you mention.

"Why are you interested in this job/career?" Surprisingly, many recent grads stumble over the response to this question. Your answer should demonstrate your knowledge of the job and industry, and why you think you would be successful in it. You want the employer to feel that you have given a lot of thought to your decision to interview with them—more than just needing a job.

"Where do you see yourself in five years? What are your short-term goals? How much money do you expect to be earning in five years?" Again, the same question. Rather than quoting a specific salary, demonstrate your understanding of the industry, salary ranges, typical career paths, rate of growth, and your desire to learn and apply your specific skills so that you can be successful.

"What are your long-range goals? Where do you see yourself ten years from now? Fifteen years from now?" I hate these questions, which make applicants feel as though they should have their entire lives mapped out. Ninety-nine percent of interviewees answer these questions with the usual blather that suggests they have planned everything out personally and professionally for fear that if they don't, they won't appear focused and ambitious. If you have planned that far in advance, good for you. However, most recent grads haven't planned beyond the weekend, let alone ten years. Demonstrate your understanding of where someone typically could be in that profession with ten or fifteen years of experience. But also acknowledge that planning ten years ahead is a long time at this point in your life, and that you want to continue making current decisions that provide you with an opportunity to continue learning and growing. This demonstrates an honest and mature thought process that any employer would respect.

"What were your most rewarding accomplishments?" Again, accomplishments should revolve around demonstrating your strengths, how you handled challenging situations and displayed initiative. Employers want to determine what your priorities are and what sort of value system you have. Are the accomplishments trivial? Do they demonstrate your interest in working with and helping others?

"What is your greatest weakness?" This question never fails to make my top-ten list of worst questions an interviewer can ask. Questions like these are what make applicants prepare for interviews as if they were tests. What are you supposed to say? "My greatest weakness is that I love to sleep and I have trouble getting out of bed in the morning," or worse, something that if you admitted would disqualify you for the job. If you are unfortunate enough to have an amateur interviewer who relies on these types of questions, then you don't have a choice but to "play the game." Steer clear of personal character traits. If you they won't let you joke the question off with an answer of "chocolate mousse" or some other indulgence, then turn the negative question into a positive answer about how you are continuing to work at upgrading skills that would benefit you personally and professionally, an answer that doesn't weaken your qualifications for the job.

"Would you be willing to travel? Do you have geographical preferences?" By all means state geographical preferences; but at this point, why limit yourself? You don't have the job offer yet. Even if you aren't willing to relocate, first find out if they want to hire you. No sense eliminating yourself by not demonstrating a willingness to be open-minded and flexible. Many attractive opportunities are available through relocation. Once you have the offer, then you can make the decision.

"What do you know about our organization? What ways do you think you can contribute? Why do you want to work here? What do you think it takes to be successful in our organization?" Essentially the same question. You are interviewing with that company, for that job, in that industry. Why? How much do you know about all of these things? How much research have you done? Why do you think you would be successful? They want to know what you know and why you've made the decision to pursue this direction. You can't stumble here. This is where your research comes in handy, and you need to demonstrate how you fit in and what you can contribute.

"What did you like least about college/last job/etc.?"

Negative questions are aimed at understanding how you view and handle adversity, challenges, and disappointment. Are you an optimist or a pessimist? Do you complain or do you look for solutions? Again, turn every negative question into a positive answer. Don't say your boss was a jerk, or that you hated your college. Discuss what you learned from the experience and the challenge, and how it has helped you. Be specific. Be positive.

"How well do you handle pressure? In what kind of work environment are you most comfortable? In what size organization do you think you would work best?" What are you going to say? "I *freak* out under pressure!" "I need solitude, a work environment where I can be left alone." Obviously you want to demonstrate flexibility, that you are someone who can thrive in a variety of settings and situations. Give examples from your own experiences of how you were able to succeed in a variety of settings. These questions are also indirect ways of exploring how much you know about the industry and how you would fit in. Show off your research and how your strengths match their organizational needs.

"What motivates you to put forth your greatest effort? What are the most important rewards you expect to find in your career? How important is money to you?" Money is important. We all need it to live so it is okay to say that. But in most professions, it isn't the *most* important reward for putting forth your best effort. Organizations value employees who demonstrate initiative and are motivated by their own values and work ethic, not carrots dangling in front of them. Illustrate through activities and work experience how and why you were motivated to put forth your greatest effort.

"If you could, how would you change your course of study/work/life?" This is a subtle negative question. Resist the temptation to discuss regrets, unhappy or unsuccessful experiences that you might change. Be positive. Everything is a learning experience and has helped to create the person you are today with the opportunities you have now. Because you are presenting yourself as someone they should hire, obviously you don't want to change anything that has helped create who you are. Demonstrate an understanding of this, and let them know you wouldn't change a thing.

By now you should have noticed a pattern. Employers have come up with dozens of ways to ask the same questions, all of which are engineered to find out whether you would be a good fit for the organization. At the same time, you should be assessing whether or not the organization would be a good fit for you. The general impressions you had and information you learned will help you determine that. However, before you make any final judgments, you should proceed with appropriate interview follow-up and accept an invitation for a second interview if one is extended. You have nothing to lose at this point, even if your gut tells you this isn't your dream job. You may not find a first job that meets all of your requirements, so you may have to take the best one available. If nothing else, going through the process is a learning experience that will benefit you when you are interviewing for that dream job.

CHAPTER SEVEN

Follow-up

Great is the art of beginning,
but greater is the art of ending.
                    —Henry Wadsworth Longfellow

Many recent grads walk out of job interviews feeling relieved and resigned, as if they had just completed a grueling final exam. After hours of preparation for the big moment, there is nothing left to do but sit back and wait for the grade. By the end of an interview, the company has already decided whether or not they are interested in you for that job. And 99.9 percent of the time, if they're not interested, there is nothing you can do to change their mind. However, if they are interested, but just haven't offered you the job yet, there is plenty you can do, or fail to do, that can prevent you from getting the job.

Take advantage of the opportunity to demonstrate your writing skills, creativity, and ability to relate to and understand different people and situations. Regardless of what decision the company has made, proper follow-up is critical for leaving a positive impression. If you aren't going to be considered for the job you interviewed for, it may help keep the door open for future positions. If you are still in the running, proper follow-up will not only help you stay in the game, but may be the tiebreaker that wins you the job.

Thank-You Notes

Immediately after the interview, exhale and take a moment to fully absorb the experience and process the information you gathered from it. Write down the general topics discussed, common personal interests, and anything that may have been unique or noteworthy about the meeting. Use that information to write a personalized thank-you note to each person you met. Double-check the business cards you collected after each meeting to make sure that you've correctly spelled names and titles. Keep in mind that there were a dozen applicants before and after you. Your ability to connect with each interviewer by tapping into the uniqueness of your meeting will leave a lasting impression.

During one interview I was conducting, the building decided to conduct a fire drill. The female fire searcher for our floor was out that day, so the candidate volunteered to search the women's restrooms on the floor. It was impressive how she handled the situation so comfortably and naturally. She mentioned the fire drill in a follow-up note, using the experience to make an analogy about her ability to "put out fires" in a crisis. Corny but effective. She got the job. Another applicant and I shared a passion for movies, which we talked about at length during the interview. Her follow-up note included a quote from one of my favorite movies that summed up how she felt about the interview and the company.

Most interviews will not be formal, strict, Q&A interrogations. More likely they will be conversational, allowing you to discuss common areas of interest. But even if you weren't *lucky* enough to have a fire drill during your interview and spent your time answering banal "where do you see yourself in five years?" questions, the basic rules for writing effective thank-you notes are the same—keep them short, relevant, and timely.

Very simply, you are thanking them for their time and the opportunity to discuss the position and the company. Reiterate one or two relevant qualifications that make you an ideal candidate. If you can convey this by relating it to a common interest or something unique about the meeting, do so. Express your interest and enthusiasm, and that's it. Two short paragraphs at the most.

Send the note the same day of the interview, or the next at the latest. You want to get it into their hands while your meeting is still fresh in their minds. However, there is no need to send it via overnight mail or messenger. It is a waste of money, especially since you may have to send out dozens of these letters.

The Handwritten or Typed Debate

As with most of the job-search process, if you use a little common sense, you will be successful. Sending a handwritten note is perfectly acceptable as long as your handwriting wouldn't interest the FBI and doesn't say anything more about you than "this is a person with legible handwriting." Some interviewers may have a preference, but it isn't going to have any impact on their decision, so don't worry about it. If you choose to type it, use a standard business letter format. Personally, I prefer handwritten notes on simple, classic note cards or stationery. It is more personal and stands out from the rest of the mail. You can also creatively use a blank greeting card that somehow relates to the situation. However, once again, keep it simple and use common sense. For example, one applicant from Chicago admired the black-and-white photographs of New York landmarks in my office, which led to a discussion about the two cities. After the interview, she sent a card with a black-and-white photograph of a Chicago landmark on the front. A simple, nice touch.

Most entry-level applicants do not send follow-up thank-you notes. Take the extra time to write them. Even just a straightforward note to say thank you, without any creative personalization, will stand out because it is rarely done. It is an important gesture that can leave a lasting, positive impression.

Pest Control

If they want you, they will call. If they don't, they will let you know. If you have to call them to remind them who you are, then they are not interested. Do not call to thank them for the interview. Do not call them to ask questions you forgot to ask during the interview. Do not call them just to say, "Hi, I'm still here and waiting, what's up?" Employers are very busy and are annoyed by these calls. Don't be a pest.

Before you leave the interview, find out the company's time frame for making a decision, and ask about the next step in the process. Send the thank-you notes immediately after the interview, and wait. If you are not contacted by the company within the time frame they have given, then you can call. While there are many possible reasons you haven't heard from the company within the stated time, frankly, it usually isn't a good sign. Most entry-level positions are filled quickly. If the company is interested, you will usually know either at the end of the interview or very shortly thereafter. Usually, only after the position has been filled will the other candidates receive their rejection letter ("Sorry, but we've found another candidate whose background was more suitable . . .").

If the anticipation is killing you, call at the appropriate time. No tricks or gimmicks are necessary. You don't have to try all of the annoying guerilla tactics for getting past the receptionist or secretary. We understand what you want to know and why it is important to you. Just be courteous and honest. If you want to reach the interviewer directly, try calling before 9 A.M. or after 5 P.M. Whether you get through directly to the person, reach voice mail, or a secretary, use the same approach: "Hello, my name is . . . , and I met with you [or X] on such and such a date to discuss the marketing assistant position. I remain very interested and was wondering if you could tell me the status of my candidacy." If you reach voice mail or a secretary, simply leave your telephone number, ask for a call back, and say "thank you."

Follow-up Intervieiws

You get the call. The first interview did go well and you made the cut; they want to see you again and maybe have you meet other people in the company. If you were excited about the job and hoped to get a call back, you enthusiastically agree to a second interview. But even if you weren't excited about the job and are having second thoughts, you have nothing to lose by meeting again. At this point in your career, even if you don't think you are interested in the job, never refuse an offer for a second interview. You may have missed something the first time around and could gain new information from someone with a different perspective that might change your mind. At the very least, you will gain valuable experience. Take advantage of the opportunity so that you'll be prepared for a second interview for a job that you *are* interested in.

If you are called back, understand that you are being considered very seriously for the position. You may be the only candidate, or one of two or three at the most. During the follow-up meeting, remember that interviewing is a two-way street. You're both measuring your feelings about each other against that first impression. If the first impression was truly just a well-prepared best foot forward for either side, it will probably be revealed in a second interview. That is why they are conducted. How is the chemistry the second time around? Is there consistency in presentation, attitude, and knowledge? Are the strengths confirmed? Are there any lingering concerns or reservations? If you do have the opportunity to meet other employees, ask them about their experiences in the industry and with the company. Try to draw a composite of the company culture to find out what it would be like to work there.

If you were properly prepared for the first interview, didn't rehearse or resort to gimmicks, you won't have to worry about re-creating an act. You'll repeat your winning performance naturally. However, repeating that winning interview performance does not mean repeating that interview's previous outfit. Three interview ensembles, if mixed and matched properly, can get you through the most active job search.

"And the Job Goes to . . .You!"

Congratulations! It is very gratifying to hear the words, "We'd like you to join our firm." Out of all of the candidates who wanted this position, they have chosen you. How does it make you feel? Your reaction is very important. Even if you expected the offer, or aren't as excited about the job as the company is about you, show enthusiasm. It is deflating for a company to go through an extensive recruiting process to find that one person they feel is right, only to have that person view the job, offer with apathy or disinterest.

Whether the offer comes in person or via the telephone, react with enthusiasm and appreciation, and thank them for the offer. Make sure to keep your cool—no screaming, hugging, or high-fiving. It is prudent not to accept on the spot unless it has been a lengthy interview process and you know this is your dream job and cannot contain yourself. Most companies do no expect you to accept immediately, and do not interpret this as lack of interest or excitement.

Obtain all the necessary details about salary and benefits, and ask for a copy of the benefits guide they provide for new hires. Most entry-level hires underestimate the importance and value of the benefits package a company has to offer. Many accept without even asking about benefits. It is impossible to evaluate the full value of a job offer or compare it to another offer without understanding the complete benefits package. For example, health insurance premiums and 401K plans can vary greatly. Don't forget to find out when the medical coverage begins. Many companies have waiting periods, and you will want to be covered elsewhere in the interim.

Ask if there is a formal performance appraisal procedure and how often salaries are reviewed. Few, if any, of these items are ever negotiable, especially at the entry level, so do not even bother trying. Often, entry-level salaries for recent graduates are not negotiable. If you did your homework, the starting salary should not be a surprise to you. However, if you do want to try to negotiate the salary, when you are being made an offer is *not* the time to do it.

Your primary goal at the time you receive an offer is gathering all the important terms so that you can fully evaluate the offer. Once this is accomplished, thank them again, express your excitement, and ask them if you can have some time to think about it. You might say, "As I am sure you can understand, this is an important decision and a lot of information to absorb. May I have some time to think about it?" They are expecting this, so don't worry, they will not take the offer away from you. You will probably be given anywhere from a few days to a week to make your decision.

Evaluating the Offer

There are a lot of factors to consider when evaluating a job offer. Are you interested in the industry, company, job? Will it provide you with an opportunity to learn and utilize and develop your skills? Do you like the people and the culture? Is it a foot in the door that could lead to other opportunities? Do you think your boss will be a mentor? These are the most important questions to ask. While it is an important decision, remember to keep it in perspective; it is, after all, only a first job. If it is not the right opportunity, do not be afraid to turn it down. You received this job offer, you will receive another.

If you want to try to negotiate a higher salary, call them back the next day and tell them that you are excited about the offer and the possibility of working for the company, but you are wondering if there is any flexibility in the starting salary. If you are fortunate enough to have offers for similar, higher-paying positions, or have interviewed elsewhere for similar positions offering more, tell them that. However, do not risk a great opportunity by being unreasonable or trying to play hardball. Ask politely. If there is flexibility in the starting salary, it will probably amount to no more than a few dollars after taxes anyway. If the salary is firm, they will tell you that. It is a mistake to let the starting salary of your first job be a determining factor. If you are excited about the opportunity, take it. Do what you love—do it well—and the money will follow.

When the Second Choice Comes First

You've interviewed with two companies. Your first choice hasn't made a decision yet, but the second company makes you an offer. What do you do? Gather all of the information about the offer and ask the company for some time to think about it, as we've discussed. Then immediately call the other company and let them know that you have received another offer, but that their company is your first choice. You will find out very quickly whether or not you are being considered for the position. If you're not, your dilemma is solved. If you are still in the running, your stock will immediately rise, as well as your anxiety. They will either accelerate their recruiting process and make you an offer before you have to respond to the other company or they will tell you that you are a serious candidate but they aren't able to make a final decision within the time frame you need. At least you will be able to ascertain just how seriously they are considering you and when they expect to make a final decision. It is unlikely that a company will keep you waiting if they aren't very interested in you, knowing that you have another job offer that you might risk by waiting for their decision.

Now what? It depends on what is important to you and how much of a gambler you are. If you ask the first company for an extension, you risk losing the offer. Asking for an extension is usually a clear sign that the applicant is waiting to hear about another job in which they are more interested. Companies do not want to be second choice. You can tell them that you just want to be as thorough in evaluating all of your options as you were in the effort you put forth to achieve those options, and you need a little more time. For this approach to succeed, you must also quickly reassure them that you are indeed interested in their company and the position. The company may not want or be able to grant the extension. They may say that they have other qualified candidates who would jump at this opportunity, and rescind the offer. While it's less likely, it may happen.

If you are willing to roll the dice and risk the offer, make sure you tell that to the other company. What action more clearly demonstrates your interest and sincere desire to work for a company than your willingness to forego a competing offer while you wait for them to make a decision? This may just tip the scales in your favor.

Thank You, but No Thank You

Employers obviously do most of the rejecting in this courtship. However, if you find yourself in the enviable position of being able to choose from several offers, then it is important to be courteous and professional when declining an offer. The company has invested a lot of time and effort in you and the entire recruiting process, and may have other qualified candidates who are waiting for a decision to be made. Furthermore, those candidates may have decisions pending at other companies. If they are no longer available by the time you finally decline their offer, the company will not have any backup candidates and will have to begin the recruiting process again.

The people who offered you a job can remain important contacts if you decline appropriately and professionally. It is possible that your paths may cross again, especially if your other job is in the same industry. Notify them via telephone of your decision as soon as you can. Explain that after careful consideration you have decided to accept another opportunity that is more suited to your interests at this time. Thank them for their time and the opportunity to meet with them. Compliment the company and the experience you had interviewing there. Follow-up with a letter expressing similar sentiments. In the future, don't be surprised if you receive a call from that same company offering you an opportunity to advance your career with it.

And the Job Goes . . . to Someone Else

The message is usually delivered via a thin envelope through the mail: "While your background is impressive, unfortunately . . ." blah, blah, blah. No matter how easily they try to let you down, the bottom line is someone else got the job and you didn't. Don't get down on yourself. The baseball player with a .300 batting average is considered an all-star even though he fails to get a hit 7 out of every 10 times at bat. No matter how often you don't succeed, remember, you just need *one* hit to be a success.

The fact that you didn't get the job doesn't necessarily mean that you did something wrong or that they didn't like you. You may have come up against stiff competition. There may have been many extremely qualified applicants possessing great backgrounds and skills applying for the job. The deciding factor may have been the chemistry with that particular hiring manager, a common alma mater, the CEO's niece, or shared interest in eighteenth-century Russian literature.

Send Another Note

If candidates rarely send notes after interviewing for a job, how many do you think send notes after being rejected for a job? Send another note to the individuals you met during the process, once again thanking them for the opportunity to meet and be considered for the position. You can say that although you are disappointed that you did not get the job, you are still very interested in the company and would like to be considered for any other positions that may become available in the future.

Anything can happen. The first person they hired may change their mind and decide not to take the position; they may quit after a week, get fired, or whatever. It happens more often than you may think. In that situation, employers frequently return to the other candidates rather than start the entire process over again. If they do reconsider the other candidates, who do you think they would call first?

Despite the advice of career guidebooks that suggest avoiding the human resources department like the plague, this department can be your most important ally. While a hiring manager may know of one or two positions available in their department, the Human Resources Department knows about *every* position available in the entire company. The senior director of staffing for Time, Inc. once told me, "If an applicant just contacts someone on a magazine, they may find out about one or two positions on that magazine. If they contact me, they will find out about 140 positions available on many different magazines."

Also, a human resources professional may see something in your background that might make you a good fit for a position that perhaps you hadn't even thought about. Because there is often enormous pressure on recruiters to refer candidates as soon as a position becomes available, they keep an active file of qualified applicants they've met and possibly referred to other jobs. If you are good, they will continue to refer you to vacant positions until you are hired within the company, give up, or are hired by another company. Furthermore, when you are hired through the human resources department, they feel responsible for you. They worked hard to bring you into the company, and they want to see and help you succeed as much as anyone does. The human resources department is also responsible for training, employee relations, protecting employees' rights, not to mention advising on career progressions, salaries, and promotions. It seems obvious that avoiding the human resources department is not only a bad job-search strategy, but a poor career strategy. This is not to suggest that you should rely solely on the human resources department to be your advocate. You should network to get to anyone and everyone who can help you locate the job you want.

PART
—TWO

Oh, The Places You'll Go

If a man is called to be a streetsweeper,
he should sweep streets even as Michelangelo painted,
or Beethoven composed music, or Shakespeare wrote
poetry.
He should sweep streets so well that all the hosts
of heaven and earth will pause to say,
here lived a great streetsweeper who did his job well.
—Martin Luther King, Jr.

In Part One we debunked job-search myths and discussed how to avoid ineffective job-search strategies and reduce, if not eliminate, the painful trial and error often experienced by the uninitiated job seeker. You are now equipped for the leap "out there," and despite what the jaded purveyors of doom and gloom say, it is *not* "a jungle out there." Dr. Seuss's *Oh, The Places You'll Go* has been on the best-seller lists for years. It is a commencement address that resonates with recent graduates because it simply, eloquently, and optimistically describes life's journey. Read it if you haven't already.

There are hundreds of industries and thousands of diverse jobs you can pursue. Remember, you are embarking on an exciting journey. While you will certainly experience your share of ups and downs, the journey is supposed to be *fun*. As a recent graduate, you are probably less encumbered now than you ever will be, so follow the only consistent advice from career counseling professionals—choose a career that you will enjoy. If making widgets or counting beans makes you jump out of bed in the morning, then do it.

As we discussed in chapter four, there are numerous resources available in print and on-line that you can turn to for information on thousands of companies in every industry. There are thorough and extensive books, as well as periodicals like the major weekly business and newsmagazines and government reports that list the top jobs, companies, and industries today and for the future. Most of these lists are compiled from institutional economic forecasts and industry trends.

The following is my highly subjective list of rewarding careers for liberal arts majors. While liberal arts graduates enjoy success at all levels of most industries, I consider these particularly exciting, fun, interesting, diverse, and creative industries and careers that especially value and require the skills liberal arts graduates have to offer. The information was compiled from my professional experiences and from those of the many colleagues and liberal arts graduates working in these fields who have been interviewed for this book.

I've targeted several specific industries that offer an array of rewarding career opportunities. I've also included specific careers that can be explored in a number of different industries. Many of the careers are in communications, those which are often considered "glamour" industries and difficult to break into. It is true that these are more competitive than most other professions, but they are not nearly as closed as the conventional wisdom suggests. Don't let your potential be bound by convention. You do not need to call the CEO Mom or Dad to get a job. The job-search strategies we discussed in Part One; the following Profiles section, which illuminates the realities of each field; and the Strategies for Getting In section are your keys to gaining admittance.

Once you get inside, a hard-work ethic, talent, and initiative are the basic ingredients for advancement and success, which is true of any industry. A little timing and luck also play a role. However, it is not a coincidence that the individuals who possess these key ingredients are frequently in the right place at the right time and have the most luck. Furthermore, these industries require a commitment far greater than a "work is what I do for a living" mentality.

To succeed in these competitive fields, your career must become one of the passions in your life. Nine-to-fivers need not apply. In many ways, these professions are extensions of a liberal arts education, in which the world becomes a classroom and you have an opportunity to become both student and teacher. They provide a natural outlet for the skills and interests of many liberal arts graduates and offer rich personal rewards that are not easily quantifiable. After reading this section, perhaps you will confirm what you already suspected about the career path right for you. Perhaps you will have an epiphany, and a career will suddenly be revealed as your calling. Or perhaps none of these careers will strike a responsive chord, and you will set your sights on a different vocation altogether.

Whatever you decide, remember that your decision need not have life-long implications. If you discover that the path you have chosen is leading you in the wrong direction, simply choose another path. The cliché that parents have been passing down to their children for generations is true: You can be whatever you want to be if you set your mind to it. It's up to you.

CHAPTER EIGHT

Book Publishing

A good book is the precious lifeblood of a master spirit— embalmed and treasured up on purpose to a life beyond life.

—*Milton*

Overview

Books were the lifeblood of your education. It is difficult to imagine a liberal arts major not loving books. Most of the books you read during college were required reading. Some you enjoyed, others you hated—but the act of reading was always pleasurable. There is an intimacy in the texture of books, and the pleasure of curling up with one has withstood every technological advancement.

Consider for a moment the remarkable uniqueness of the medium in an age dominated by broadcasting, cable, movies, and the Internet. Books are personal, portable, and transferable. They require no power source, yet project voices and images that can be replayed on the big screen of your imagination an infinite number of times.

While books consumed a substantial portion of your budget and time during your academic career, you might not have considered them as a professional career. Many students don't. The business of book publishing is not an academic discipline widely taught in college, unlike journalism or magazine publishing. Yet in many ways publishing is a business like any other. IBM makes computers, The Gap makes clothes, and publishers make books. At the same time, book publishing is unlike any other business, and therein lies its mystery and its magic.

Book publishing defies conventional business logic. Publishers do not simply manufacture a product assembled by workers in a factory. The product publishers sell is the unique, personal, intellectual property created by one owner, the author. Significant capital and overhead is invested in deciding *which* books to publish, *how many* copies to print, and *how to* publish them. However, these decisions are not based on scientific data or sophisticated market research. The decisions are subject to the personal likes, dislikes, creative talents, and guesswork of the many individuals involved in the process. And while publishers strive for distinction in a particular publishing genre, most consumers remain oblivious to the publisher when they buy books; they select books based on an author or subject matter. The success of any publishing program is often dictated by an unpredictable and mostly undefinable marketplace. Many books do not earn a profit, yet each year the industry funnels approximately 50,000 titles into the marketplace, hoping the few will pay for the many. Some are the "big" books with high advances, large print runs, and huge marketing budgets that you expect to sell well, though sometimes they don't.

Others are the smaller books published with less fanfare and lower expectations that sometimes become surprise hits because of word of mouth, fortuitous timing, or rave reviews in the media. This is what makes publishing a risky business, and an intensely exciting and creative one.

Most people think of publishing only in terms of authors, editors, bookstores, and the *New York Times* best-seller list. The type of books that most people are familiar with, such as fiction, biography, history, art, music, self-help, business, humor, current affairs, cookbooks, etc., comprise what are called adult trade books. These books account for only about 15 percent of the industry's revenues. In addition to the adult trade books, there are children's books, which include picture books and books for young readers of various age levels sold to stores and libraries;

university press books, which are published by the universities to which many of the authors are affiliated and include general interest books as well as those serving the specialized needs of academia; elementary and high school textbooks, which include workbooks and teacher's manuals sold directly to schools; college textbooks; reference books; religious books; mass market books, which are the rack-size paperbacks typically associated with romance and mystery genres; and technical and scientific books, which include specialized works for professions such as medicine and law.

One of the most appealing characteristics of the industry is the variety of the career opportunities it has to offer. Annually, book publishing is a $21 billion industry that employs approximately 75,000 professionals involved in each phase of building the bridges between authors and readers. It is not exactly a giant industry, especially if you consider that some corporations are larger than the entire book publishing profession combined. But the quaintness of the industry is part of its charm, where publishing firms are called "houses," and professionals consider themselves members of a community. What better home for a liberal arts graduate? Book publishing is an industry that offers a stimulating environment where interesting, intelligent, creative individuals share their talents and experiences to create books on every conceivable topic for millions of readers.

Many recent graduates enter the field embracing the idealistic, romantic notion of literature and book publishing as a noble endeavor. But realistically, publishing requires a constant balancing act of respect for the written line and the bottom line— which makes it no less fun or respectable.

Career Profiles

A book publisher has many departments vital to its operations, such as accounting, royalties, contracts, administration, human resources, operations, and technology. While these department offer rewarding career opportunities, they usually aren't the primary attraction for recent graduates entering the profession. The areas that offer the most compelling career opportunities for recent graduates are editorial, managing editorial, production, subsidiary rights, publicity, and sales. While the structure and job descriptions may vary depending on the house's size and field of specialization, the essential responsibilities are consistent. Each job plays an important and distinctive role in the process of getting the book from writer to reader, and the following descriptions will help you to determine where to apply your particular interests and skills.

Editorial

Editors are the primary link to the submissions—manuscripts and proposals—that publishing houses consider for publication. They need to understand the entire publishing process because they are usually involved in all phases of the book's production. Editors must be voracious readers and have a sense of what interests people. Their primary responsibilities are to help shape a house's "list"—the books they publish each season—by reading and evaluating submissions and making recommendations about what material should be acquired. Successful editors do not just wait passively for projects to cross their desks. They constantly search for new writers and material and generate their own ideas for books.

An editor's success is based on the quality of the projects he or she can bring to the house and his or her business sense—the ability to pick material that in the aggregate can earn a profit. When considering a manuscript or proposal, editors must determine whether or not the writing style is acceptable, whether the topic has been covered before, whether the author can pull off the project, whether there is a market for it, whether it is the right fit for the house, and, finally, whether it's economically feasible. Editors frequently turn to individuals from other departments within the house to determine whether or not a book is worth acquiring.

When a project is acquired, an editor's role shifts to helping the author write the best book possible and galvanizing the other departments to generate maximum support to insure the book has the best possible chance for succeeding. This is important because the other departments play a critical role in the success of a publishing program.

Managing Editorial

Sometimes called editorial production, this department keeps track of all of the schedules and manages the flow of materials between all of the departments. This requires incredible organizational skills and attention to detail. Depending on the size of the house and its list, there could be anywhere from a few to hundreds of books in the pipeline at various stages of completion. Manuscripts must be put on a schedule so that production, design, marketing, publicity, and sales can coordinate efforts to produce, market, and sell the completed book. Deadlines also help the author finish the book. (Trust me, I know!) Managing editors also coordinate the work of copyeditors, who check the completed manuscript for proper spelling, grammar, punctuation, and syntax.

Production

The love affair people have with books stems not just from the content but from the tactile pleasure of the book's craftsmanship—its look, feel, and smell; the quality of its paper and binding; its type style and the way the text is designed on the page. This is why, despite what the "revolutionaries" for a paperless world predict, books will continue to survive in their current form. Production is where all of these elements that you love about books come together, and the finished product is crafted by coordinating the work of designers, printers, and binders. Production is also responsible for estimating costs of manufacturing books based on the design and print specifications, as well as maintaining each book's budget. Spend one day in this department, and you will never look at books the same way again.

Subsidiary Rights

The subsidiary rights department is responsible for licensing to other publishers and media outlets the right to use the company's intellectual property in specific formats—for a fee, of course.

There are a variety of channels rights personnel have at their disposal for maximizing revenues through licensing. Books originally published in hardcover can be sold to publishers who will reprint the book in a less expensive paperback format. Serial rights allow books to be excerpted in newspapers, magazines, and other periodicals. Other reprint rights are sold to foreign publishers and book clubs. Translation rights are sold to foreign language publishers, and audio rights to publishers of books on cassette. Technology is creating new channels for generating additional revenues from electronic rights. Sometimes when a book project stimulates a buzz within the publishing community, it creates a high demand for licensing rights that can ensure the profitability of the book before it is ever published and regardless of how well it sells. Revenues obtained from any rights deals are shared with the author according to the terms of the contract.

Publicity

Because advertising in major media outlets is so expensive, most houses rely on more cost-effective publicity campaigns as the primary means for creating awareness and stimulating interest in their books.

Each title challenges the publicist to find the hook that will enable them to pitch the book and the author to key players in the media. Publicists develop their strategies months in advance of a book's release. Depending on the subject matter and the author, a combination of techniques are employed to trigger the media's attention. Advance copies, press releases, and promotional pieces are sent to book reviewers, gossip columnists, radio and television producers, reporters, editors of periodicals—anyone who has access to the public and can promote the book. Publicity campaigns can help make or break a book, and timing is crucial.

Because competition for shelf space in bookstores is fierce, most books have only a small window of opportunity to get noticed once they go on sale. Campaigns usually begin just prior to the launch of a book to generate anticipation, then hit in full force once the books land in the stores. Campaigns also include setting up press parties, author tours, and book signings. Publicists must know the authors, books, and media well in order to plan an effective campaign that strategically targets appropriate media outlets. Excellent oral, written, and interpersonal communication skills are critical to a publicist's success.

Sales

The word is anathema to most liberal arts graduates. It usually conjures up images of Willy Loman in *Death of a Salesman*. However, the job of the sales representative in book publishing is unlike the responsibilities of a salesperson in any other profession. They have defined territories and customers who actually get upset if they aren't visited regularly, because their livelihood depends on what reps have to sell.

While most functions in the publishing process are designed to get books *out* of the bookstore, sales reps are responsible for getting books *into* the bookstores. To help reps position books effectively and meet the sales objectives for each title, publishers hold sales conferences about three times per year. This is where management and sales representatives from all over the country come together to discuss the upcoming season's titles and their sales handles. Since sales reps are closer to the bookstores and the book buyers than anyone else in the organization, their feedback is encouraged on each book's cover design, title, and management's sales goals.

After a sales conference, reps are prepared to do more than just show up and present the company's new titles. They act more like consultants and inventory managers. Armed with promotional materials and marketing information, the sales reps help bookstores determine which books to buy and in what quantity, based on each store's particular customer base and sales history with various titles. At the same time, they are trying to achieve management's sales expectations. Sales professionals are some of the most knowledgeable, well-read individuals in the book publishing industry.

Entry Level

Take the name of each department described in the preceding pages, add "assistant" to it, and that is the entry-level job for the department. The job description? Typing, filing, answering phones, photocopying, mailing. Repeat it like a mantra. You didn't spend four years in college and go deep into student loan debt to do clerical work, you say? Then book publishing is not for you. While most people are attracted to the industry because they love books, that love is put to the test in the first few years. Entry-level jobs are characterized by long hours and hard work, but not much pay.

This reality weeds out many recent graduates in the interviewing process, and even more in the first year on the job. The entry level is a dues-paying apprenticeship. There are no shortcuts to the top. However, being in the publishing environment as someone's assistant allows you to learn a tremendous amount about the industry just by osmosis. You must see beyond the clerical work and distill from the mundane that which is special and unique to your role. Since there is no formal training program, a boss willing to be a mentor to you is critical to the development of your career. But ultimately, your success is up to you. You are hired for what you know and for your potential. Your curiosity, initiative, and ability to learn are the keys to success in an entry-level position and the keys to getting promoted *out* of an entry-level position—usually after one to two years. However, the careers of most publishing professionals, like the process of publishing a book, do not necessarily follow a structured, linear progression. You do not have to start out in editorial to become an editor. In fact, in textbook publishing, most employees are required to start in field sales in order to learn the business before moving on to other departments.

You can spend the first few years exploring different departments if you have the opportunity. Just don't let too much time pass before you find your niche or it will be more difficult to make a switch. The experience and skills obtained in one department don't necessarily transfer at the same level to another department. For example, a senior publicist wouldn't know a thing about production. Wherever you start, learn as much as you can about the entire business, not just the role of your department. This knowledge will help you perform better in your job and accelerate your rise within the publishing ranks.

Career Progression

While each function has a specific career track one can follow, the rate of advancement is unpredictable and is not guaranteed. Editorial usually has the longest apprenticeship and slowest track because it is the foundation of the business. It takes time to learn the business and demonstrate your talent and commitment well enough for management, agents, and authors to have the confidence to trust you with their intellectual property and the responsibility for shaping a house's list. It can take five years or longer to become a full editor if you have the talent.

Advancement can be quicker in other departments, but requires no less commitment and talent. In all functions of book publishing, career advancement typically means gradually and consistently taking on more responsibility and autonomy. This growth is reflected in higher titles and pay, as you'll see in the next section. If your career remains stagnant for more than one to two years during the first five years, something is wrong. Career mobility is a characteristic of the industry. It is common during the early stages of one's career to move out in order to move up. It is equally common to return to the company where you began your career.

Typical Career Track Titles

Unlike most other industries, book publishing is very hierarchical, as the job titles that follow demonstrate.

EDITORIAL

Editorial Assistant, Assistant Editor, Associate Editor, Editor, Senior Editor, Executive Editor, Editorial Director, Editor-in-Chief

MANAGING EDITORIAL

Assistant to the Managing Editor, Assistant Managing Editor, Associate Managing Editor, Managing Editor, Executive Managing Editor

PRODUCTION

Production Assistant, Production Associate, Production Coordinator, Production Supervisor, Manager, Director

SUBSIDIARY RIGHTS

Subsidiary Rights Assistant, Rights Associate, Assistant Manager, Manager, Director of Subsidiary Rights

PUBLICITY

Publicity Assistant, Associate Publicist, Publicist, Senior Publicist, Publicity Manager, Associate Director, Director

SALES

The career track for sales reps usually involves taking on larger, more important territories and accounts, or responsibility for a region and other reps as a Regional Manager. Sales positions also often lead to positions in management at the home office such as Field Sales Manager, National Accounts Manager, and Director of Sales.

Salaries

It is a myth that publishing professionals must take vows of abject poverty. The industry has come a long way since the days of $11,000 per year starting salaries. Average entry-level salaries are now approximately $20,000 per year, which isn't going to buy you that new Mercedes, but can be manageable with creative budgeting. While salary ranges during the first few years in any of publishing's primary functions are usually fairly standard and predictable, publishing is not known for its formal compensation practices and structure. Advancement can be tortoise- or rabbit-like, depending on how quickly and often you get promoted, change jobs, or distinguish yourself as a "star." I've witnessed people ten years into their careers earning $40,000 per year, and other individuals who were earning $150,000 after five years, although both are exceptions. Salary ranges also depend on the type of publishing, size of the company, and geographic location. Average salaries of adult trade editors in New York City, those with best-selling big-name authors, can vary widely in the six-figure range, while editors of academic books at small university presses can vary widely in the mid-five-figure range.

Someone once told me that if you earn at least your age in thousands of dollars annually, then you are doing better than most people in the country. If you use that formula as a yardstick, you may be playing catch-up early on, but will probably match your age within a few years. Doubling your age in salary at any point in your career puts you in a better position than most in the industry. Tripling or more, and congratulations, you are among the top of your profession!

Strategies for Getting In

Here's where you can tailor the job-search strategies we discussed in Part One to publishing or the specific job you are applying for. Obviously, any directly related experience should be high-lighted on your résumé and emphasized during interviews. Be creative. You probably have more related experience than you realize. If you were involved in college fund-raising or planning events, that would be very relevant to a job in publicity or promotions. If your interest is in children's publishing, let them know you have worked with or tutored children. The majority of recent graduates applying to the industry are initially focused on editorial. While this makes competition for those jobs even stiffer, it means there is less competition for the other jobs.

If you do not want editorial, broadcast that like a neon sign. Other departments are always pleasantly surprised when candidates target them specifically. If you do want editorial and haven't been able to find a job, setting your sights on another department increases your opportunity to get your foot in the door. It is much easier to find the job you want when you are inside the industry. Just don't let anyone know that they are your second choice, of course. (I know what you are thinking, but it is only a little white lie.) And who knows, once you experience a different department, you may discover that you actually would prefer to pursue that path.

Admitting that you love books during the interview is fine, and usually expected, but make sure to acknowledge that it is a cliché, and instead demonstrate a deeper understanding of the industry and your reasons for being attracted to it. Turnover at the entry level is high, often due to the disillusionment some new hires experience when faced with the day-to-day realities of the job.

Because of this, hiring managers view applicants for entry-level positions with a degree of skepticism. Anticipating and alleviating an interviewer's concerns by articulating your understanding of the realities of the industry, the entry-level job, and what it takes to succeed will give you an edge over the other applicants.

Applicants who are short on experience, or who aren't having much success in their search, should work in a bookstore at least part-time, or volunteer if necessary. Publishing companies *love* that kind of experience, and it may rejuvenate your search. You will be able to make new networking contacts within the bookstore and may have direct interaction with sales and marketing representatives from various houses. The experience will also provide you with an introduction to the industry from a different viewpoint.

If you continue to have difficulties locating a job, or would like to learn more about the industry before applying for jobs, then I strongly recommend that you consider one of the summer publishing programs offered at a number of colleges around the country. These programs vary in length from four to seven weeks and offer a crash course in publishing taught by working industry professionals. They are not cheap, costing anywhere from $3,000 to $5,000, but they are worth the price of admission for the networking contacts alone. The placement rate for the graduates is usually very high.

The most popular programs are:

The Radcliffe Publishing Course
6 Ash Street
Cambridge, MA 02138
(617) 495–8678

University of Denver Publishing Institute
2075 South University, No. D114
Denver, CO 80210
(303) 871–2570

The NYU Center for Publishing
11 West 42nd Street, Room 400
New York, NY 10036
(212) 790–3232

The Rice University Publishing Program
School of Continuing Studies—MS 550
6100 Main
Houston, TX 77005
(713) 527–4803

The New York University Center for Publishing also has a continuing education program dedicated to publishing, as well as a masters degree program. Pace University in New York also offers a masters degree in publishing. However, an advanced degree is unusual and is not required for a career in the industry.

While the competition for jobs can be fierce at times, have faith. If you are committed to getting a job in publishing and persistently employ these job-search techniques and insider strategies, you *will* find a job.

What Insiders Say

This depends on when you ask. Because the first two years are the most volatile in terms of turnover, you are likely to hear as many voices of discontent as you do those singing the praises of the industry. However, junior staff with either perspective share one common complaint the wages: "Ridiculous," "Depressing," "Have to work a second job to supplement my income". Assistants have also said that they resent processing their bosses' expense reports and learning that they earn less than what their boss spends on lunches. There are just as many assistants who are excited to be working with books and interesting people, even though the pay is low and the hours are long. Everyone unanimously loves the casual dress code and relaxed atmosphere, especially assistants who remind you that they could not afford to buy a business wardrobe on their salary. Not surprisingly, positive comments begin to outweigh negative ones the longer people have worked in the industry. Five years out or more, professionals have usually settled into a niche and frequently say they couldn't imagine doing anything else for a living.

General Information

PRIMARY INDUSTRY PUBLICATIONS:
Literary Market Place (LMP)
Comprehensive directory of the American and Canadian book publishing industry. Available in the reference section of libraries.

Publishers Weekly
245 W. 17th Street
New York, NY 10011
(212) 463–6758

PRIMARY INDUSTRY ASSOCIATIONS:
Association of American Publishers (AAP)
71 Fifth Avenue
New York, NY 10003
(212) 255–0200

Association of American University Presses
548 Broadway, Suite 410
New York, NY 10012
(212) 941–6610

American Booksellers Association
828 South Broadway
Tarrytown, NY 10591
(914) 591–2665

QUICK TIPS FOR BREAKING INTO BOOK PUBLISHING

1. Research the company's current and backlist titles that you can refer to when applying for a job. You can obtain copies of their catalogs from the sales or customer service department.
2. When interviewing, never say that you only enjoy reading the classics, or criticize a particular genre of books published today.
3. If you are interviewing for an editorial assistant position, you will probably be given a manuscript to read and evaluate. Hand deliver a 1 to 2 page readers report the next day even if they give you a week to complete the assignment.
4. Consider entering the business as a literary agent's assistant. You can find a complete listing of agents in the LMP.
5. Be prepared to discuss favorite authors and books you've read that have been published recently.
6. Read the *New York Times Book Review* and know what is on the bestseller lists before the interview.
7. Apply to one of the Summer Publishing Programs if you can afford it. The placement rate for graduates is extraordinary and the contacts invaluable for your entire career.
8. The Lynne Palmer Agency may be able to help if you are looking for a job in the New York City area. They specialize in publishing, and place people in positions at all levels in the industry—(212) 883-0203.

CHAPTER NINE

Magazine Publishing

A magazine . . . is an experiment and represents a new focus, and a new ratio between commerce and intellect
—*John Jay Chapman*

Overview

Having visited college campuses and publishing programs over the years, I have met thousands of liberal arts graduates interested in pursuing a publishing career. Invariably, whenever I ask for a show of hands of the students interested specifically in book publishing, arms fly into the air. The students are as proud as peacocks to pursue a career so steeped in education and literature. On the other hand, the students preferring magazine publishing seem to have an inferiority complex in the company of those pursuing such a noble endeavor. Their arms are half raised, crooked at the elbow, seemingly weighed down by society's higher esteem for books. Their complex is rooted in the stereotype that books are literature, permanently enriching the culture, and that magazines are inferior, disposable, trendy. This is a stereotype rooted in myth. While books are generally held in high regard, one need only look at the breadth of titles in the bookstores and on the best-seller lists to realize that most fail to qualify for their exalted status.

Alternatively, some of the most respected authors often write for magazines. Furthermore, magazines often prove to be the best medium for new writers to demonstrate their literary prowess. The truth is, magazines are as diverse as all the genres of books published. They help us keep our finger on the pulse of current events in the worlds of business, sports, news, fashion, health, politics, and entertainment, to name just a few.

Magazines are also an important part of your cultural education, offering political and social commentary from a variety of perspectives. Some magazines are even prominently displayed or collected, like *Architectural Digest* or *National Geographic*. Magazines are economical. You can get a year's subscription for the same cost as a hardcover book. Magazines are fun, fast, easy to use, portable, and attractive, and the print doesn't smudge on your hands. You are allowed to crimp the corners, fold them, or cut out the pages if you like. Try doing that with a book, then call me after you have been burned in effigy. Magazines also get you through some stressful moments, because what would we do without them while waiting to get our teeth drilled, suffering through long lines at the supermarket, and anxiously anticipating an interview in a reception area?

For career potential, magazine publishing is also not nearly as northeast-centric as book publishing. There are a broad range of regional and national publications published in cities all over the country. Most magazines are divided into two general categories, consumer and trade. There are over 14,000 consumer magazines such as *People, Cosmopolitan, Esquire,* and *Vanity Fair,* which appeal to a wide general audience. There are more than 4,000 trade magazines, such as *Publishers Weekly, Broadcasting Magazine,* and *Variety,* which are not generally available on the newsstand because the content is narrowly focused to a particular industry. Trade magazine must be subscribed to. There are also numerous small literary and academic journals, which are usually funded by universities and nonprofit foundations.

Magazines have flourished for 250 years in our country. Each year, approximately 300 new magazines are launched, each hoping to inform and entertain readers. While only a small percentage of upstarts survive, newcomers are rarely dissuaded by the statistics. So go ahead, rejoice in your decision to pursue a career in magazines.

The industry offers diverse, rewarding opportunities, many in some of your favorite subject areas. And I'll tell you a secret: In private, many of the "book" students admit that they would work in magazines, too, if they were offered the chance.

Profiles

Separation of church and state is widely observed in magazine publishing. Most major publishers are divided into two equally important but distinct groups, business and editorial. Each has its own masthead that lists the various departments and contributors responsible for creating the publication. They each work independently of the other, and they rarely have a say in the other's activities. Sometimes the two divisions aren't even located in the same city.

The editorial division of *Architectural Digest,* for instance, is located in California; its business division is located in New York. At smaller magazines, the functions usually overlap. Not surprisingly, most liberal arts majors think of editorial when considering a career in magazine publishing. The word "business" alone is anathema to many. However, the business of producing a magazine is also creative, and it generally offers more career options with greater opportunity for advancement than editorial. The business side is also less competitive to break into, and it usually offers higher financial rewards.

Sometimes there is an undercurrent of competition between the two divisions as to which actually controls or drives the magazine. Usually, though, they respect each other's contribution and dedication to producing the best publication possible because it couldn't happen without their combined efforts.

Business

Advertising Sales

Magazines are a business and depend on advertising to survive. While revenue is derived from subscription and newsstand sales, the bulk of the revenue for both consumer and trade magazines comes from advertising. Consumer and trade magazines generate more than $11 billion of advertising annually. The department responsible for bringing in that revenue is advertising sales.

Most magazines develop rates that they charge for different-sized ads based on their circulation. Advertisers usually engage the services of advertising agencies to help them determine how and where to spend their advertising budget. The magazine's sales representatives develop relationships with advertisers and the media planners at the agencies to convince them to advertise in their magazine.

Competition for a piece of an account's advertising budget is stiff, not only from other magazines but from other media. Therefore, sales reps must develop an intimate knowledge of the industry and each advertiser. Sales reps usually specialize in categories such as automotive, apparel, tobacco and liquor, fashion, and food, because advertisers in each have unique needs and markets. Successful reps are familiar with an account's audience, their own magazine's demographics, and the demographics of the competition.

Armed with marketing and research data, sales reps make presentations to different accounts using their knowledge to convince them that their publication is the right environment for their product.

Sales Promotion

The sales promotion department is responsible for creating the printed materials that sales reps use to sell the magazine. Promotional materials might include new surveys about the demographics of the magazine's readers and the client's consumers; graphs of the buying habits of consumers; announcements of special awards, increased circulation, and anything that might convince an account to advertise in the magazine.

Research

A magazine must have a distinct voice and personality. It must identify its target audience and what its demographics are—age, gender, income, purchasing habits, etc. This helps to shape the design and look of a magazine, its editorial content, and how it is sold. None of this can happen without the research department. They are responsible for compiling, coordinating, and analyzing existing and potential markets by evaluating surveys, projections, and demographic trends in society. The creative use of this information by the sales promotion department can help sales representatives position the magazine against the competition and define an image that an advertiser would want to be associated with.

Circulation/Subscriptions

As we have discussed, in order for most magazines to survive, they must sell advertising. The amount of money a publisher charges for different ads, called their rate card, is primarily based on their circulation numbers from both subscription and newsstand sales. That makes this department a critical player on the team. It is this department's job to increase copies in circulation by means of various direct mail and marketing campaigns. They are responsible for the "junk" mail you receive at home. Your name boldly emblazoned on sweepstakes entry forms, letters with stamps to lick and paste, pitch letters "personalized" to you about how your "discriminating" tastes fit the profile of their readers, and calls from telemarketers offering unbeatable values are the work of this department. They are also responsible for those annoying little "blow in" cards that fall out of every other page until you finally decide to fill one out. After all, there is no postage necessary and you can always opt for being "billed later." Sneaky, but very effective.

Promotion

Not to be confused with sales promotion, this department creates "events" that advertisers can participate in. These events are designed to boost the image of both the magazine and the advertiser. Fashion magazines may sponsor fashion shows in department stores across the country that feature the clothes of their advertisers. Food magazines may conduct food- and wine-tasting events at various culinary institutes and trade shows. These creative programs provide added value because they enable the magazine to offer exposure for their advertisers without the additional cost of advertising.

Publicity

This department is responsible for ensuring that the events and activities of the magazine get mentioned by the media. Whether it is news of promotional events, contests, awards, or special issues such as the *Sports Illustrated* swimsuit edition, or *Time*'s "Man of the Year," the publicity department uses its contacts in the media to get the attention. Sometimes it is the notoriety of a writer, editor, or publisher of the magazine, or controversy about an article or cover that will help generate additional exposure for the magazine.

Editorial

The editor-in-chief determines the direction and content of the magazine. This includes supervising the art, design, layout, cover, and text. Their job is to choreograph all of these elements to give the magazine a personality and style that its readers identify with. The editor must make sure the magazine's voice consistently reaches its readers, yet infuse each issue with fresh content and concepts that maintains the readers' interest and loyalty. Magazines are usually organized into subject departments—fashion, news, entertainment, fiction, business, etc.—depending on the type of publication. Each department is headed by an editor who coordinates the activities of that area. The editorial staff usually works on several issues at a time, under the supervision of the editor-in-chief.

While magazines vary in type and frequency, the process of producing a publication is generally the same. Typically, an issue begins with a general meeting with the editorial staff, writers, photographers, and art directors several months ahead of publication date. At this meeting, the staff will brainstorm to decide on the theme for the issue, subjects for articles, and discuss ideas for the cover. Readers expect their magazines to stay on the cutting edge, which is the editor's greatest challenge, especially when planning issues months in advance.

During a second meeting with the heads of each department, final decisions about the theme and editorial content are made. Articles are assigned to editors and writers, and assignments are also made for art and photography for the inside pages and the cover. Most magazines operate on a fixed ratio of advertising pages to editorial pages, so the editor must work with the publisher to estimate how many pages of advertising they expect to sell for that issue.

Regular meetings with the various departments occur as the issue begins to take shape. The editorial staff coordinates and guides the work of writers, shaping the articles and columns to their final form. Lower-level editorial staff may fact-check and proofread articles, while the art director's staff may coordinate photo shoots, conduct cover conferences, and prepare artwork and photos that will run with the articles. The editor-in-chief appraises and approves the work in progress of several issues simultaneously.

Before an issue is put to bed, the editor-in-chief scrutinizes the final page proofs with all of the elements in place. This is the last chance to make final changes. Once approved, there is no time to rest as the focus immediately shifts to the magazine's next issues.

Newsmagazines are primarily driven by current events, so they are particularly susceptible to late-breaking news that may affect the publication. The editorial staff is always on high alert as they prepare to put the magazine to bed, knowing that should a major event occur they may have to "crash" a revised issue in order to remain current. However, if a choice ever has to be made between revising an issue to remain timely and making deadline, meeting the deadline *always* wins.

Juggling all of the elements of several issues simultaneously is the job of the managing editor. He or she orchestrates the efforts of the editorial, art, and production departments to ensure that all the deadlines are met. They also oversee the copyediting and fact-checking staff to ensure that each article and issue is grammatically and factually correct.

Entry Level

A liberal arts background is invaluable for a career in any of the functions profiled. You must be a voracious reader, a competent writer, naturally curious, and have excellent communication skills. The entry-level positions are apprenticeships. Your on-the-job training involves assisting with the various responsibilities of the department. These include fact-checking, compiling sales kits and research data, coordinating the logistics of a promotional event or photo shoot, trafficking materials, reading, evaluating, and responding to submissions from freelance writers, answering phone calls, and making a lot of photocopies.

You must be able to juggle many projects simultaneously and be meticulous about details. Most important, you must be able to do all of that successfully under deadline pressure. Just as in show business—the show must go on—the magazine must make deadline. Round-the-clock hours may be required to get the issue out. If you are to be successful in the magazine business, you will need to consider that part of the appeal rather than a burden.

Career Progression

Climbing the ranks is harder and takes longer on the editorial side than on the business side of the magazine. There is a talent that editors possess that can not be taught. What distinguishes editors is their feel for the subtle nuances of both visual and writing style. Many editors also plan and write features and articles themselves, depending on the type of magazine. Therefore, excellent writing skills are required. The track one typically follows with time is assistant editor, associate editor, editor, senior editor.

On the business side, recent grads can start out as sales reps for smaller, regional magazines. Otherwise, they may start out in a sales support capacity, learning the business before taking the next step—actually calling on a few small accounts. A salesperson's career is built by developing relationships with bigger accounts and hopping to magazines with increasingly larger circulations and profiles. Career advancement for a sales rep can be meteoric. Some people prefer the flexibility and lifestyle of sales and stay in it their entire careers. For those who want to move up into management, the next step is ad sales manager or director. They manage the entire ad sales department, set policy, and are accountable for attaining the advertising sales goals of the staff. The next and final step is the publisher, who oversees the activities and sets the agenda of all of the business-side departments.

Career advancement in the other departments follows a more traditional and predictable path. Talented individuals will gradually receive more responsibility and can grow into management positions in their respective areas. Magazine publishing is a predominantly youth-oriented industry, with many individuals skyrocketing to executive positions in their early thirties.

Salaries

Salaries vary widely depending on the type and size of the magazine and region of the country. You can expect approximately $20,000 at the entry level. The first few years are usually marked by slow, gradual increases. However, after that, salary advancement matches the rate of increased responsibility, which can be rapid. Publishers of major consumer magazines can earn as much as $300,000 to $400,000 annually, more if incentives and perks are included. It is not uncommon for department heads in other areas to earn salaries in the low six figures. Sales reps can also earn over $100,000 per year. Editorial salary ranges are slightly lower. Copyeditors average $30,000 to $40,000, and department editors may earn twice that amount. However, the editor-in-chief of a major consumer magazine can earn as much as their publisher counterparts.

Strategies for Getting In

Magazines make it very easy for you to network. The mastheads list the structure of the departments, with the names and titles and sometimes phone numbers of most of the employees. Try to get some internship experience before you graduate. But even if you have already donned the cap and gown, many magazines will still allow you to apply for an internship. Highlight any related experience including participation in school publications on your résumé. If it is buried on the bottom, create a separate publishing experience section.

Do not focus on the glamour aspect of the business during interviews. Demonstrate your respect for the medium and the various roles it can play in our society. And don't forget to consider the less glamorous departments. As we have discussed, there are many more facets to producing a magazine than editorial. Once you are inside, if the other departments aren't your cup of tea, you can always transfer.

The field is competitive but not impossible. Do not limit your options by focusing only on the prominent publications. Only a few entry-level positions become available each year on those publications. There are nearly 20,000 consumer and trade magazines across the country. They offer a multitude of exciting career opportunities and more room for advancement than the handful of high-profile magazines.

Most of the summer publishing programs devote their time equally to books and magazines, and therefore are recommended highly for breaking into the business, although it should be noted that they are by no means required for entry into the publishing profession. They offer excellent networking opportunities, and the graduates from each program historically have enjoyed high rates of success breaking into the industry. For many, these facts make the $3,000 to $5,000 tuition worthwhile.

The most popular programs are:

The Radcliffe Publishing Course
6 Ash Street
Cambridge, MA 02138
(617) 495-8678

The NYU Center for Publishing
New York University
11 West 42nd Street, Room 400
New York, NY 10036
(212) 790-3232

The Rice University Publishing Program
School of Continuing Studies-MS 550
6100 Main
Houston, TX 77005
(713) 527-4803

What Insiders Say

Most professionals in magazine publishing experience high career satisfaction. This is especially true of trade magazines. This can be attributed to the fact that individuals at trade magazines usually have an expertise or particular interest in the specific subject matter or industry the publication serves. Trade magazines employ more than 100,000 people, and although most publications do not appear on newsstands, they have more than seventy million readers.

It is difficult to deny the appeal of the high-profile consumer magazines. Most find the fame by association fun and stimulating. Assistants, however, in every creative industry complain about the low pay, long hours, and clerical work. Yet many say that the gratification of seeing the tangible results of their efforts makes it worthwhile.

Fashion magazines generate the most polarized views. Many enjoy their work because it is fun, light, and "most women love this stuff." However, one dissenter said, "They [the employees] are all vapid, Calvin Klein–model wannabes. They take hemlines, makeup, and accessories so seriously, sometimes you just want to smack them." Ouch!

Whether or not fashion is your passion, career satisfaction is generally high in the industry, especially for those who have made it past the first few years and whose input directly affects the shape, style, and success of the publication.

General Information

PRIMARY TRADE PUBLICATION
Folio
Cowles Business Media
470 Park Avenue South
7th floor, North Tower
New York, NY 10016
(212) 683-3540

PRIMARY INDUSTRY ASSOCIATION
Magazine Publishers of America
919 Third Avenue
New York, NY 10022
(212) 872-3700

QUICK TIPS FOR BREAKING INTO MAGAZINE PUBLISHING

1. Demonstrate your ability to work well under pressure with examples from school, work and extracurricular activities.
2. Be prepared to discuss why you like the particular publication you are interviewing with, and other favorite magazines. It is fine to admit that you also enjoy a competitor's magazines—it is likely that the interviewer has worked at other publications.
3. Prepare different functional résumés that highlight your specific skills, interests and experience that relate to the focus of each publication you are applying to.
4. Consider working for an in-house corporate newsletter.
5. With the internet growing by 300,000 pages each week, many corporate web sites have evolved into sophisticated interactive on-line magazines. Consider applying to companies in any industry that interest you, in the division that is responsible for coordinating, writing, editing and designing the content of the website.
6. Apply to one of the Summer Publishing Programs if you can afford it. The placement rate for graduates is extraordinary and the contacts invaluable for your entire career.
7. The Lynne Palmer Agency may be able to help if you are looking for a job in The New York City area. They specialize in publishing, and place people in positions at all levels in the industry—(212) 883-0203.

CHAPTER TEN

Retailing

> *Commerce is the great civiliser. We exchange ideas when we exchange fabrics.*
>
> —*R.G. Ingersoll*

Overview

You might be thinking, "Retailing? Greg, you have got to be kidding!" Dedicate my life to stocking shelves and ringing up merchandise for rude shoppers who treat retail employees only slightly better than department of motor vehicle employees? Or work in an environment that forces you to swallow your pride daily because the customer *isn't* always right (the birthplace of the phrase "I want to speak to a manager") or where it doesn't matter what the tag says, because they found it hanging on the clearance rack? You say you did the minimum-wage holiday-rush gig to make pocket money during college, but you didn't study humanities to make it a career. "No sale," you say? Think again. Retailing offers many diverse and exciting career opportunities that may be the perfect accessory to your liberal arts degree. Retail is big business—to the tune of $2 trillion annually and twenty-five million jobs. These are not just jobs on the front lines, facing the assault of the public, but interesting, creative jobs that require imagination and vision. It is also a field to which you can bring insightful, firsthand experience. Everyone is a consumer.

In the simplest terms, retailing is the business of providing goods and services to the public. But retailing is much more than that. It is a creative business of learning how to appeal to consumers' needs and desires. Retail professionals draw on their knowledge of sociology, psychology, and history to understand what drives current trends and to forecast the direction of consumer buying habits.

From the trading outposts of the frontier to the mass-market chain stores of today, the retailing landscape has evolved and grown dramatically over the past 200 years. These changes reflect many of the socioeconomic forces that have transformed our nation and help to illuminate the complexity and diversity of this dynamic industry.

The general store of the frontier was the cornerstone of retailing. Owners stocked a wide assortment of general goods, like 7-Elevens, without the slurpees. As the population and manufacturing grew, general stores evolved into specialty stores such as clothing, shoes, and hardware shops, providing a wider variety of a particular product. Specialty stores sprouted up next to each other, creating Main streets, the first American shopping centers. In the mid-1800s, retailers capitalized on the needs of a growing nation and launched department stores like Woolworth. Department stores offered greater variety than general stores, with the convenience of specialty departments at discounted prices, all under one roof.

Today, the trend towards "bigger is better" continues with the growth of Warehouse Shopping Clubs and specialty chain stores. There is a Gap or Benetton on practically every corner and in every shopping center, and chains such as Wal-Mart and K-Mart stand as monoliths of consumerism across the country.

The way we shop continues to evolve as retailers respond to changes in marketplace forces and consumer habits. Aided by advancements in technology, retailers strive to deliver products to the public more efficiently and less expensively, in increasingly creative ways. While traditional non-store retailing, such as mail-order catalogs, continues to thrive, the success of QVC, the Home Shopping Network, and online shopping demonstrates retailers' creativity and ingenuity in redefining shopping environments and expanding their markets.

Retailing is critical to our nation's economy. While corporate America merges and downsizes, the retail industry continues to expand in every region of America. With baby boomers in their peak earning years, the population exploding, and 1.4 million new graduates like yourself with new credit cards burning holes through their pockets, the industry has a healthy future. As you can see, retailing is much more than checking to see if there's a size 4 blouse in the back—it's a cutting-edge career choice for the twenty-first century.

Career Profiles

While retailing varies greatly across the country, from small boutiques to chain superstores, the titles and functions of the various jobs in retail are generally the same. Retailing, like any industry, has support functions that keep the business running, such as human resources, operations, administration, and finance. Each of these areas offers interesting career opportunities. However, merchandising, sales promotion, and retail operations are the three functions that comprise the core of the industry. They define the industry and are the primary attraction for recent graduates interested in pursuing a career in retailing. A general overview of each is provided below.

Sales Promotion

Every store needs to promote itself by communicating with the public. Everything from advertising, publicity, in-store events, special promotions, window displays, interior design, and decorations can fall under the purview of sales promotion. The Macy's Thanksgiving Day Parade and Fourth of July fireworks display are two prime examples of event sponsorship that the promotion department will use to bring attention to a retailer. However, most promotional activities are smaller in scale. These might include generating store themes; redecorating the interior to reflect the changing season; and organizing picture-taking with Santa, fashion shows, cooking demonstrations, and free giveaways. Promotions and/or events that help generate awareness in the store and build customer enthusiasm and loyalty are the primary responsibility of the sales promotion department.

Retail Operations

This generally includes the sales staff, merchandisers, and store managers. Even if you have never performed a tour of duty in a store, you know just by being a consumer that the sales staff is the public face of a retail operation. Their primary responsibility is customer service. They restock the display floor, answer questions, find the right size or color, ring up merchandise, and, depending on the type of operation, sells by presenting products and features. Some staff work on commissions. You can usually identify employees working on commission if they shadow you, offering to hold your merchandise while you continue shopping, nearly pulling it out of your hands.

Merchandisers are generally responsible for the design and layout of the store. In all aspects of retailing, product placement and display have a big impact on customers' buying habits. Supermarkets never place the staples—bread, milk, and juice—in the aisle nearest the entrance. They make you walk through the store, past the cookies and chips, in order to reach the eggs, so that you will be tempted to buy the nonessentials. The next time you are in a multilevel department store with escalators, notice that you have to walk around to the other side of the floor to catch the next escalator continuing in your direction, maneuvering you to pass racks of merchandise.

Store managers are responsible for the day-to-day operations of the selling floor. They supervise and motivate the sales staff, ensure guidelines and policies are met, resolve disputes, and control the sales floor inventory of merchandise.

Merchandising

Merchandisers in retail operations are basically responsible for creating the store environment and the display of merchandise. However, the merchandising department is concerned with the actual merchandise. And the person around whom all retailing revolves is the buyer. The buyer's job is essentially to seek and select the merchandise that a store will sell. It is a powerful and often glamorous job, but requires hard work and long, erratic hours. Buyers frequently travel to fashion shows, trade shows, and industry conferences both in the United States and abroad, examining manufacturers' lines, negotiating prices, and purchasing what their experience, instincts, and market research tell them will sell in their stores. It is an exciting but pressure-filled job because the decisions a buyer makes, including the color, size, quantity, and price of merchandise, often determine whether a company makes a profit. Buyers' mistakes show up on clearance racks.

Entry Level

Most large retail organizations have formal training programs that expose trainees to all aspects of the retail operation. Training programs often begin with classroom instruction in the fundamentals of retail operations. Trainees also receive on-the-job experience by working in each area of the organization on a rotational basis. The training programs are often grueling, involving hard work and long, irregular hours. Weekend and evening shifts are common, and the entire program can last anywhere from one to several years, depending on the organization. Training programs are usually very competitive because retail organizations select individuals for their potential executive ability. Trainees are usually groomed for positions in merchandising and retail operations and are constantly evaluated by management. Aptitude for the field, excellent customer service attitude, analytical and communication skills, enthusiasm, initiative, and stamina are all required for successful completion of most training programs and advancement into management positions.

While direct entry into a training program is the most effective way to break into retailing and learn about the business, it is not the only way. Many smaller retail operations do not have formal training programs. Starting out means accepting any job within the organization, taking the initiative to learn every aspect of the business, and demonstrating the same skills required for success in a training program.

Career Progression

Trainees who successfully emerge from the training program are placed on a career track that enables them to focus on a particular aspect of retailing. Those interested in merchandising start out as assistant buyers and handle a variety of clerical tasks that generally lighten the heavy load of the buyer such as processing orders, checking the status of merchandise delivery and inventory, and keeping track of markdowns and items that need to be returned to the manufacturer. Assistant buyers' duties vary as they gain experience and may include traveling with the buyer, suggesting merchandise that might be considered for the department, and presenting new items to the sales staff.

Promotion to buyer can occur within a few years, which is a key executive position in the organizational structure. Buyers are under enormous pressure, constantly grappling with decisions about merchandise, quality, styles, prices, consumer buying habits and trends, orders, reorders, and product merchandising, all while trying to motivate the sales staff. Some individuals love the excitement and prestige of selecting a store's merchandise and prefer to remain at this level. Others with many years of successful buying experience advance to more senior management positions such as divisional merchandising manager and general merchandising manager. Merchandise managers responsibilities include coordinating the activities of a group of buyers from related departments, setting sales goals, deciding markups and markdowns, and establishing sales promotions. They may travel extensively, researching new markets, manufacturers, and suppliers, helping their buyers stay on top of the most current information and trends. Merchandise managers establish and control the budgets their buyers have to work with and are responsible for helping the organization meet its sales and profits objectives.

After the training program, a retail operations professional generally starts as an assistant store manager eventually moving up to store manager, with responsibility for the day-to-day operations of a store, within a few years. Depending on the size of the organization and number of outlets, store managers can advance to district and regional managers with responsibility for an increasing number of stores, before climbing into a senior management VP position. In smaller organizations, it is not uncommon to start as a salesperson before climbing into an assistant manager and manager role.

Jobs in the sales promotion departments—publicity, advertising, promotions—often begin at the entry level as an assistant and progress with a gradual increase in responsibility from general clerical work to the actual design and implementation of programs and events. Typical titles include associate, coordinator, assistant manager, manager, and director.

Salaries

Many sales personnel make slightly more than minimum wage to start. However, trainees in formal programs usually earn between $22,000 to $28,000. Talented individuals are rewarded with promotions and raises. Base salaries are usually supplemented with sales incentive bonuses and can vary depending on the size, type, location, and profitability of the operation. General salary ranges for store managers, excluding bonuses, are usually $35,000 to $60,000. District and regional managers come closer to six-figure salaries, and vice presidents can earn well in excess of $100,000 per year. Salary ranges on the merchandising side of the business are generally higher, with many experienced buyers with proven track records earning $100,000 or more. Senior merchandising managers who have been successful buyers can earn twice that amount with sales incentives. Salaries for the sales promotion jobs are the lowest of the three divisions, but still climb on average to the high five-figure range at the top of advertising, publicity, or promotions departments.

Strategies for Getting In

Let's face it, getting a job in retail doesn't really require a strategy. Walk into any retail organization that interests you and apply for a job. Ideally, though, you want to start in a training program; but you can't just walk in and get one of those positions. They are usually very competitive, with many talented recent graduates vying for limited spots. Applicants must demonstrate enthusiasm, a sincere customer-service attitude, and flexibility because it is a dynamic industry that requires you to perform a wide variety of tasks and interact with diverse people on a daily basis. Recruiters also want to see examples of your decisiveness, analytical skills, and stamina because the work conditions often include long hours, irregular schedules and require quick thinking under pressure. Retailing is a powerful economic force in our country. You can stay current with business trends by reading the *Wall Street Journal* and the "Selling" section of *Fortune* magazine.

Some training programs have rigid start dates that coincide with May and December graduations. Others have floating start dates throughout the year. Apply for one of those positions through listings at the career development office of your college or by contacting the human resources department of any major retail organization. If the timing is off or you aren't selected for one of those coveted spots, apply for a job working in any department of a retail organization. Don't underestimate the value of this kind of experience. You will have an opportunity to get a feel for the industry and to compare your own interests and qualifications with the requirements of the business. Furthermore, once you are inside, you can demonstrate the skills that will get you noticed and help you secure a position in the next training class.

Finally, contact the National Retail Institute at (202) 783-0370. This nonprofit foundation conducts research and education programs for retailers, and individuals interested in pursuing a career in retailing. They also provide detailed information on the various career opportunities within the industry, how to find them, certification programs, and a program of scholarships for college students pursuing careers in retailing.

What Insiders Say

Reviews on the industry are mixed. According to one junior-level employee, "Retail management requires a rough skin because people are rude and irrational." "Customers don't appreciate what you do for them. Go elsewhere," says a senior executive. Dissatisfaction seems high for career sales people, but those pursuing careers in management as buyers or store managers usually have survived rigorous training and are enjoying the freedom from the rigid walls and schedules of corporate America. Buyers seem to love what they do. They thrive on the pressure and the excitement (says one buyer, "There is an art and science to selecting merchandise—it's addictive"). Many store managers enjoy the diversity of their job responsibilities and the unpredictable challenges they face every day with the public. They say that interacting with different people is stimulating, and working on a sales floor is both mentally and physically challenging. Enjoying customer service is a key factor for happiness in the industry, and most professionals also note the deep discounts on products as a great perk.

General Information

Primary Trade Associations
National Retail Federation
325 7th Street NW
Washington, D.C. 20004
(202) 783-7971

National Retail Institute
325 7th Street, NW, Suite 1000
Washington, D.C. 20004
(202) 783-0370

QUICK TIPS FOR BREAKING INTO RETAIL

1. Emphasize rather than apologize for your part-time work experience as a cashier, waiter, bartender, or salesperson.
2. Emphasize your innate customer service ability through examples in work, school and extracurricular activities.
3. Be prepared to discuss in an interview what motivates you as a consumer.
4. Never criticize the competition. You don't know where the interviewer may have worked before, or where you or the interviewer will be working in the future.
5. If you are unsuccessful gaining entry into a retail management training program, apply for any job within any large, retail environment that interests you. Tell the interviewer it is your intention to learn the business and move into management eventually. It will set you apart from 99% of the applicants.

CHAPTER ELEVEN ——————

Television

I hate television. I hate it as much as peanuts. But I can't stop eating peanuts.

—*Orson Welles*

Overview

Television is the most glamorous and dominant mass-media industry. It is a socially powerful medium that touches virtually everyone, whether as an educator, entertainer, or companion, and we've been glued to its screen for over fifty years. Approximately 99 percent of all U.S. households have at least one television, and as a nation we watch an average of seven hours of television programming per day. No matter where we live, or what our socioeconomic background, a touch of a button transports us all to a common community. Together we watch historical events unfold across the globe, and we all have our favorite shows and characters, around whom much of our social conversation centers. Most people know the story of the "lovely lady, who was bringing up three very lovely girls," better than they do any Dickens' tale.

For much of television's history, our viewing choices were basically limited to what was provided by the three major networks: ABC, NBC, and CBS. With the proliferation of cable and satellite broadcasting, however, the number of channels and networks has grown exponentially. The average household now receives over thirty channels with specialized programming in sports, business, health, cooking, shopping, news, weather, public affairs, movies, religion, music, education, arts, science, and dozens more.

As the number of cable stations, networks, and television stations continues to grow, so too does the demand for additional programming to fill all this air time. That bodes well for career opportunities in television all across the country. However, for a medium so predominant in our lives, the inner workings of television stations and the industry as a whole remain obscure for most people. Most think of television only in terms of celebrities and inaccessible glamour jobs in New York and Los Angeles. While most of the news and entertainment programming we see nationally does originate primarily in those two cities, there is an extraordinary amount of local programming produced all over the country, offering career opportunities in a wide range of areas.

But in order to fully comprehend the scope of career opportunities television has to offer, you must first understand the structure and expanse of the industry. If you are going to work in television, you need to know how television works.

Commercial Television

The major networks are headquartered in New York City. They supply news and entertainment programming like *20/20, Late Night with David Letterman,* and *Seinfeld* to network-owned or -affiliated local stations around the country. Affiliated local stations carry programs supplied by the network part of the day, and buy or produce their own news and entertainment programs to fill the remainder of the day. Local independent stations are not network affiliated. They buy or produce all of their own programming. There are more than 1,500 independent production companies, as well as regional and specialized program networks, that supply local stations with a variety of news, entertainment, and special-events programs. All commercial television stations sell advertising time to pay for the cost of the programming and running the station.

Public Television

The Public Broadcasting Service is a nonprofit corporation

that provides national programming for approximately 300 public stations around the country. Most of the local public stations also produce their own programs with the help of government and private funding and corporate sponsorships. Unlike commercial stations, they do not sell advertising time.

Cable Television

Developed in the 1940s to aid reception in rural areas by means of a wire, cable television has revolutionized the industry. Now, more than 60 percent of homes are wired for cable. It has become the primary means of delivering the exhaustive amount of programming produced by specialized networks like MTV, HBO, Lifetime, A&E, and CNN. Many local cable stations around the country also have their own production facilities for creating original programs. It is predicted that by the year 2000, more than 80 percent of the country will be wired for cable.

Television is our society's information and entertainment center. And as the public's appetite and the industry's need for programming on every conceivable subject grows, so too do the opportunities for liberal arts graduates. It is an industry where your career is defined by your contributions to it, not your title.

Career Profiles

Because of the industry's lack of structure, almost every career in television develops differently. If you need predictable career paths and formal job descriptions, this is not the field for you. But while duties may vary from station to station, the basic job descriptions are transferable across most broadcast and cable stations, regardless of size or network affiliation. It is common for one person to wear many hats in smaller stations. Most of the jobs in television are behind the scenes, but while they don't have the same recognition and glamour factor as the on-air jobs, they play a critical and fun role in the business of making television. Because they merit a separate discussion, news-related jobs are covered in the chapter on journalism.

Station Manager

The station manager is the boss. He or she has responsibility for the day-to-day management of the station and for making long-range plans. The station manager will have final say on all matters relating to the station's operation, such as budgeting, supervising advertising sales, hiring on-air talent, and making programming decisions. However, there are other executives reporting to the station manager who are primarily responsible for each of those areas.

Program Director

The responsibilities of the program director are to select, buy, and schedule all the local and national programming that the station broadcasts. This could include network shows, reruns of popular shows, and independently produced programs such as *Oprah* or *Jeopardy!* These shows differ from the network-produced shows that you usually see in prime time. Everyone in the country sees the network-produced *60 Minutes* on a CBS station on Sunday nights at 7 P.M. An independently produced show like *Oprah,* however, is sold to individual stations across the country at a certain price; it is up to that station to decide when to air it. That is why when you travel, you may notice that a show you are used to seeing at home at 4 P.M. on an ABC station is on at 9 A.M. on a different station in another city.

Program directors also will work with staff or free-lance producers to develop local news and entertainment programs for their stations. Their role is critical because they determine the station's lineup the way networks determine each season's schedule. Success or failure depends on ratings and advertising revenues derived from them.

Sales Manager

All commercial stations sell air time to advertisers to make their profits. They derive revenue not only from the sale of spot announcements but also from program sponsorships and from the allocation of specific time periods to the networks if they are affiliated. The sales manager prepares sales forecasts, hires, trains, and supervises the local sales reps and the national sales representatives responsible for selling and servicing accounts beyond the local area. Smaller stations may utilize the services of national sales rep firm to sell and service national accounts. The sales force may sell to sponsors directly or may work with the media department of advertising agencies representing larger sponsors who seek exposure in their particular local market.

Public Affairs Director

Television stations are chartered to broadcast in the public interest. A public affairs director maintains liaisons with local clergy, schools, community organizations, businesses, government, law enforcement, and social services to understand the issues affecting the viewers in the broadcast area. This person may write and broadcast public service announcements and editorials and may suggest local programming or coverage of special events that are in the community's interests.

Promotion/Publicity Director

This person is responsible for promoting the station's image, programming, and on-air talent. He or she may write promotional pieces and press releases announcing awards and new programs, organize promotional campaigns, and work with advertising agencies. The promotion department may also work with the other departments to coordinate or sponsor special events within the local community.

Producer

Producers are ultimately responsible for all aspects of creating a program or covering a special event. They manage budgets, hire talent, approve scripts, and direct the work of everyone involved in the production, from celebrities to technicians. Basically, producers call the shots from concept to the rehearsal and the actual broadcast to ensure that everything runs smoothly. They must have a firm grasp of all aspects of television production and be able to juggle many responsibilities under daunting time pressure. Large, live shows like *Good Morning America* and the *Today* show have many associate producers who are responsible for creating each segment of the show. Except in the case of breaking news, the segments—whether an interview with a politician, celebrity, or author—are usually produced days or weeks ahead of time. Research information on the subject is compiled, relevant videotape is reviewed, and pre-interviews are conducted by the segment producer with the guests to determine what they will talk about and how they will respond to various questions. All elements of the segment are then pulled together and timed. A research packet with the pre-interview questions and answers, planned introduction of visuals, background information, and any other pertinent data is given to the show's on-air talent the night before so they can prepare. This preplanning helps to ensure that the segment is interesting and runs smoothly, tightly, and on time. That is the mark of a good producer.

Director

While the producer is in charge and ultimately responsible for the quality of the broadcast, most of his work is done before the actual taping or live broadcast of the program. Once the show begins, it is placed in the hands of the director. The director is the person who sits in the control room in front of a wall of television monitors, choreographing all of the elements of the broadcast. He gives instructions to the camera operators and stage manager, calling for certain shots and rolls of tape.

The director is flanked on both sides by a technical director and an assistant or associate director. The technical director pushes the buttons on the console that carry out the director's commands. The next time you watch a program, notice how many different camera angles there are and how quickly they change. Each one is a push of a button in anticipation of the director's command for the appropriate shot. The assistant or associate director will keep track of the show's time and act as a second set of eyes for all of the elements that need to be introduced into the broadcast, including countdowns to and from commercial breaks, roll of tape, and graphics to be superimposed on the screen.

There Are Many More

Camera, lighting, video and sound technicians, graphic and makeup artists, tape editors, researchers, and traffic coordinators. It all depends on the size of the station. Most stations in large markets are heavily unionized. Almost every area has a representative group limiting the diversity of job functions any one person can have. But in small markets, the camera operator may also be the writer and the producer. The station manager may also sell advertising, write broadcast copy, or any task that may need an extra hand. The key to a successful career in television is enjoying doing whatever it takes to make it happen.

"Making It Happen"—Inside the Entry Level

Entry level in television is about "making it happen" at all costs. I learned this when I worked in television early in my career. I was lucky to have had the opportunity to start as an intern for a major network. I worked for Joan Lunden of *Good Morning America*. I learned of the position because Joan's manager's dentist was the husband of the associate chair of the speech department where I was finishing my graduate degree at NYU. That's not networking, however—just dumb luck and a cavity.

The biggest hurdle I had to overcome was the fact that one of the intern's responsibilities was helping Joan in the dressing room. I won the job by convincing her that my experience accompanying my mother on long shopping trips as a child had taught me how to keep my eyes closed. (Honestly.) I wasn't paid, but it didn't matter. I had the privilege of working inside a major show and network with a top star. Most people aren't that lucky. But the scope of my responsibilities and what I learned from listening to and watching professionals—what it takes to make it in the business—is transferable to anyone who wishes to pursue a career in television.

I opened fan mail, answered phones, got lunch, retrieved shoes from the dressing room, made copies, helped with the research on Joan's autobiography, and reorganized her videotape library. The interns working around me in other departments were performing equally *important* roles. But most of us performed those duties as if the show's ratings and everyone's careers depended on it. The internships of those who didn't treat their assignments the same way ended early. Take whatever responsibility they give you, no matter how small, and do it better than it has ever been done before. That is how you get noticed. Joan told me that was the best piece of advice that Barbara Walters ever gave her.

Production assistant is usually the entry-level job in television. They do everything and anything. All of the usual clerical work, and then some—type scripts, compile research and videotapes, coordinate graphics and slides, pick up people at the airport, check facts. They are involved in every detail of every component of the program from concept to completion. They do it with a high degree of thoroughness, accuracy, and dependability. The position also requires you to maintain a positive attitude and high energy, sometimes for sixteen hours a day.

My internship led to a position working for Joan's production company, which produced her cable television show and commercials. My salary was $375 per week, and I would have taken less. I didn't have *a* title: I had twenty. I performed routine secretarial work one day, and wrote treatments for show ideas that were pitched to the networks the next. When we were in production, I worked sixteen-hour days.

When you are taping shows on a deadline, it is a frenzied environment. Everything doesn't always go as planned. And when it doesn't, you have to think fast on your feet and do whatever it takes to just get the job done. It doesn't matter how big or small the problem is: "make it happen." If the fan that blows on the fake tree in the background of the scene to make it look real breaks, volunteer to twist your body under the stage and shake the tree for half an hour so you can continue taping the show until a new fan is found. If there isn't any sausage for the cooking segment that is coming up in ten minutes—find sausage, make sausage—whatever it takes. The talent and initiative to "make it happen" with a positive attitude and energy under pressure is what it takes to succeed in the business. It is also what makes it fun.

Career Progression

Almost everyone starts as an intern or assistant with a salary that ranges from $0 to $22,000 per year. Where you go from there is up to you. Television is a creative industry without rigidly structured lines of progression. The opportunity to move into any aspect of the industry depends on your interest, aptitude, and initiative.

Advancement in the industry can occur rapidly. Production assistants who distinguish themselves for their ability to pull hundreds of different technical and creative elements together accurately under pressure can become writers or producers of major network programs by the age of thirty. Promotion, programming, and sales assistants all have the opportunity to distinguish themselves in the day-to-day operations of their particular areas and can grow into management positions just as quickly.

What might be considered job hopping in another industry can be a way of life in television. Advancement for many professionals occurs when they move to positions in larger markets. If you want to work in a top market such as New York, Los Angeles, or Chicago, you can focus your efforts in those cities first. However, your networking and job-hunting skills and determination will be tested. Most people start in smaller markets, then stay or move, depending on what is important to them. There are over 200 Nielsen markets that blanket the country. There will be opportunities in and around any area you call home.

Salaries

All of the factors influencing career progression have the same effect on salary. The early years will be lean years wherever you go. Individuals at the top of their profession in any of the career profiles we discussed can earn from mid-five-figure salaries to mid-six-figure salaries. Station managers are among the highest-paid television professionals across all markets, earning on average from $50,000 to $200,000 per year. Producers and directors in small markets usually earn less than the station manager, but in larger markets they can be among the highest-paid professionals at the station. Producers of top national shows can also earn $200,000 to $300,000 per year. Directors are paid approximately half that. The salaries of sales professionals can also climb as high as anyone in television depending on sales objectives, incentive bonuses, and commissions. Basically, as your career develops, your salary usually reflects the market size.

Strategies for Getting In

Insiders unanimously agree that without some type of broadcasting or electronic media internship, college radio or television experience, or some other media experience, your search will be much more difficult. If you have already graduated and haven't had any media experience, don't worry, it's not too late. If your alma mater has a radio or television station, go back and volunteer if possible. It won't turn down an alum in need.

You might try another college in your area that has a campus station. This is a lot easier than trying to get an employer to hire you without experience. Also, take a continuing education course in any of the electronic media areas. This will give you some experience to put on your résumé and may provide you with a few inside contacts. Just be prepared to take an unpaid position if it means acquiring the experience you need.

Many people come calling because of the glamour factor. However, many aren't serious enough about a career in television to do what it takes to get a job or succeed in the industry. Recent graduates are frequently too passive in their search. They try the mass-mailing approach, hoping to get a call back. They too easily accept "sorry" or worse, no response, attributing it to television being a competitive industry. Industry professionals, who are continually swamped with résumés and telephone calls from new graduates pledging their dedication to the industry, know this. In response, many have become conditioned to saying no or not responding at all, just to be left alone. Persistence is the key. *Very* politely, *very* professionally, with humility but determination and a sense of humor, do not accept "sorry" or no response when networking for jobs until they threaten to call the authorities to make you leave them alone. Many people have been successful by just showing up at a small market station and asking to speak to someone about a job, volunteering to sweep the floors or do whatever it takes to get in. These techniques are more tolerated and accepted by creative industries than by corporate America, where you would be carted away by security. When interviewing, leave out the word "glamour" and distinguish yourself by articulating intelligent reasons why television is important and interesting to you. Allay their fears about what you might be expecting in a starting job.

Contact your local community cable station. The law requires cable operators to provide a public access channel and production facility for members of the community to produce local programming. They are almost always in need of volunteers.

Read *Broadcasting* magazine. It is *the* trade magazine for the industry. *Broadcasting's Yearbook* has a directory that lists addresses and personnel of television and cable stations around the country. Personnel change quickly, so call to make sure the person is still there and double-check the spelling of their name before sending your résumé. If you are interested in production work, include production companies in your job search. There are now over 1,500 independent production companies creating original programming for television shows for stations all over the country.

The University of Missouri's journalism department, a widely respected program, has created a Web site with invaluable current information about television markets, trends, profiles, careers, and contacts: http://www.missouri.edu.com. Another Web site, http://www.tvjobs.com, lists job openings primarily for journalists at stations all around the country. The jobs may not be appropriate, but it is a great source for names and addresses of professionals who are currently hiring at stations around the country.

The basic job-search techniques discussed in Part One, modified accordingly, will be successful if you are persistent and willing to go where the jobs are.

General Information

Primary Industry Publications

Broadcasting and Cable Magazine
245 W. 17th Street
New York, NY 10011
(212) 645-0067

Broadcasting and Cable Magazine
1705 DeSales Street NW
Washington D.C. 20036
(202) 659-2340

Primary Trade Associations

National Association of Broadcasters
1771 North Street NW
Washington, D.C. 20036
(202) 429-5300

National Cable Television Association
1724 Massachusetts Avenue
Washington, D.C. 20036
(202) 775-3669

QUICK TIPS FOR BREAKING INTO TELEVISION

1. Apply for a job as a page at one of the networks in a major market. It is one of the best entry-level jobs in the industry.
2. Send your cover letter and résumé to the station manager. If you are unsuccessful, apply in-person for any job at a small, local station. You won't be able to get past security at a large station.
3. Consider applying to video production facilities where you can learn many transferable skills, and make contact with individuals from the television industry.
4. Many advertising agencies have their own production facilities or departments that work with outside production companies to create radio and television spots. Consider this avenue for breaking into the business.
5. Read the trades such as *Variety* and *Backstage,* and contact the local chamber of commerce for information about production companies shooting programs or commercials in your area.

CHAPTER TWELVE

Journalism

Journalism will kill you, but it will keep you alive while you're at it.

—Horace Greeley

Overview

"Congress shall make no law . . . abridging the freedom of speech, or of the press . . ." Few professions have charters that are as historically based, socially significant, or passionately defended as journalism. And few professionals are as symbiotic with liberal arts studies as journalism.

From our country's earliest days, colonial journalists fanned the flames of the American revolution. Journalism has played a significant role in American history, and continues to do so. With the invention of radio, journalism broke free of the confines of newspapers, and its influence grew stronger as the dramatic events of the nation and the world were brought into millions of homes as they happened. Edward R. Murrow inspired thousands of would-be journalists with live broadcasts from London during World War II, punctuated with sounds of air sirens and exploding bombs. The era of television opened even more horizons for the profession. Journalists were now able to bring the world to the public with compelling sounds *and* sights—from the tragedies of war to the triumphs of space exploration.

Today, we live in an information-rich world, in which technological advancements have given us the capacity to access more information than ever before. But for all of technology's sophistication, effective communication of information is still a distinctly human art. Journalists are in a sense social scientists. The universe is a laboratory in which they study and report on topics from arts and entertainment to business and real estate.

The journalism profession is a calling, much like teaching. Journalists are educators and storytellers. You do not enter it for fame, fortune, or glory. Too many would-be journalists are more interested in becoming the story instead of reporting the story. If you want to be famous, try your hand at show business instead. That is not to say that there isn't an element of ego and show business in journalism. Journalists enter the world theater every day and have the power to shape the audience's perception of events as they see fit.

Over forty million people read newspapers each day, fifty million read magazines each week, and more than 100 million watch television or listen to the radio every night. By their words and actions, journalists hold the public's trust. At its highest level, journalism performs as society's watchdog, ensuring the delicate system of checks and balances remains intact. At its lowest, journalism serves its own agenda instead of the public's. Fortunately, competition makes journalists vigilant over each other, and independent groups keep an eye out for fairness and accuracy.

Journalists must be careful that their biases do not creep into their work, consciously or subconsciously, as they serve as society's gatekeepers of information. They decide which stories to cover and how much time or space to devote to each. If a prominent publication like the *New York Times* decides to run a story on the front page, the story will receive national attention. The choice of photos or footage to run with a story can also influence the public's perception. During an election year, a newspaper's endorsement of a candidate may appear not only overtly in the editorial page but also subtly with flattering photos of its candidate or unflattering shots of the opponent that run with coverage of the campaigns. Though some journalists have the power to build icons and topple presidents, only a handful of professionals make it to national prominence—breaking national stories, battling with presidents, and hobnobbing with celebrities. They represent a small percentage of the more than 100,000 professionals who bring important, relevant news to much smaller audiences throughout the country.

You might be wondering what your chances in journalism are if you have already graduated with a liberal arts degree without having taken a journalism course. Well, Edward R. Murrow majored in speech, Dan Rather went to a teacher's college, and Peter Jennings, the number-one-rated national news anchor, was a high school dropout. The Accrediting Council on Education in Journalism and Mass Communication recommends that "students obtain a comprehensive background in government, political science, economics, history, geography, sociology, at least one foreign language, English, literature, and writing." Sounds like an outline of your college transcript, doesn't it? There are unlimited issues and events to cover in the world. Journalism is not just a career or a craft—it is an intellectual pursuit.

Career Profiles

There are thousands of television and radio stations across the country with more than 40,000 professionals serving their local communities. News divisions of television stations can have as few as twelve to fifteen employees or as many as several hundred, depending on the size of the station. The news staff of radio stations also depends on the size of the station and the format— music, all news, talk, or combination. Local news programming, including sports and weather, is increasing around the country because the news division is a profit center for the overwhelming majority of broadcasting stations.

In print journalism, there are more than 58,000 people working in more than 1,700 daily newspapers around the country. Newspapers too are profitable business, capturing more advertising revenue than any other medium, including television. Two-thirds of all adults read at least some part of the newspaper every day, and the same number watch television news at some point during each day. For all of the significant differences between the print and broadcast media, newspapers and television news departments are structured in similar ways. Both are set up as information-gathering, writing, editing, and reporting centers. There are television news directors who serve the same function as a newspaper's managing or city editor. Reporters for both industries go out on assignments, compile information, and write and edit stories. Both types of reporters work on tight deadlines. The difference is that broadcast reporters face a camera and communicate the story live, or come back and edit tape and do a voice-over for later broadcast. A newspaper reporter's story appears in print in the paper.

Reporters

Most journalists are tenacious, self-motivated, and likely to work long, irregular hours. Most start in small markets, whether in print, broadcast, or the wire services, and cover everything from crime to community board meetings, sports, entertainment, and politics. Reporters in larger markets may specialize in one area. Reporters generate stories either through their own sources or from assignment editors.

Reporters must be literate and educated, and have a consuming curiosity and a "nose for news," that is, the ability to accurately assess the significance of small details and incomplete information, sense what is relevant, and put it into perspective. Reporters must have excellent researching skills so that they can find information quickly and efficiently under pressure. They also must develop and rely on sources for their stories and information.

The most important trait that all successful journalists must possess is the ability to write. The ability to write clear, powerful sentences that tell the story completely within the confines of the medium is a rare skill, and one that will secure your place in the industry. Watch your local or national news tonight. A typical thirty-minute broadcast (minus commercials, banter, and graphics) has approximately fifteen minutes of news. The number of words used to describe all of the news stories covered in those fifteen minutes is typically less than one news article. On average, a reporter has only ninety seconds to tell an entire news story. Print journalists have a different challenge. They have to produce much more copy when writing news articles, but the essence of their story must be told in the lead paragraph. It is the old who, what, when, where, why, and how—in thirty-five words or less. Journalism writing must be easy on the eye and easy on the ear.

News Directors/Managing Editors

News directors or managing editors in broadcast and print, respectively, are responsible for the day-to-day management of the news operation, including the image, format, and content of the show or publication. They are also responsible for hiring and firing and managing the news operation budget. Their jobs are frequently dependent on the ratings or circulation of the news operation they run.

News Editor/Assignment Editor

News editors assign stories to particular writers or reporters. They may edit copy, coordinate scripts, and make sure deadlines are met. They also direct the work of photographers and video editors and may decide which photos and footage will run with articles and reports.

Copyeditors

This position is particular to print journalism. After the story has been approved by the news editor, copyeditors check for errors in spelling, grammar, and punctuation. They also check the story for style to make sure it confirms to the paper's standard format. Copyeditors keep an eye out for libel and inaccuracies.

Newscasters

More commonly known as "anchors," these individuals are the personalities with whom most viewers are familiar. Ratings are more likely to affect an anchor's job than a reporter's. Contrary to popular opinion, most anchors are not simply "pretty faces." They are usually journalists who have done stints as writers and reporters and are noted for the ease with which they deliver the news. This is the coveted position in television news because it has the most visibility, glamour, and financial reward. Most people watch the same newscast each night because they are comfortable with the anchor's style and delivery. Watch the three different broadcasts of the national nightly news with Peter Jennings, Tom Brokaw, and Dan Rather. Most of the stories they cover are the same, but their styles are distinctly different. Peter Jennings projects a glamorous, slightly show business–style. Tom Brokaw has a very calm, easygoing manner, in stark contrast to Dan Rather's serious demeanor and machine-gun delivery.

Wire Services

The world's top two wire services are the Associated Press (AP) and United Press International (UPI). They are an indispensable part of the press structure. Almost every news organization is connected to the wire services, which supply news to the various media from places geographically beyond their coverage. Wire services maintain bureaus in every major American and foreign city, employing reporters who cover the news in that location. The bureaus feed news into the wire service headquarters, which then distributes the stories to the media across the country. If you check your newspaper, you will notice that articles written by staffers have bylines, and the ones from the wire services will just say AP or UPI.

Entry Level

It is possible to start as a reporter in print journalism if you have had an internship or published writing experience that you can show in the form of clips. These could be from an internship or a school newspaper.

Reporters for the wire services usually start out as "stringers." Stringers are the backbone of the wire services, working in anonymity to cover the news from the smallest counties across the nation. Stringers feed stories into the nearest bureau from places that might not otherwise get reported. That is how something of interest from an obscure location—like a farmer who grew a twenty-pound tomato or child who gets rescued from a backyard well—gets covered in major newspapers and national broadcasts.

It is also possible to start as a reporter in broadcasting, but it is much more difficult and always requires a demo tape of you covering a story. It doesn't have to be a high-quality production. They just want to see how you look and sound on the air and how well you construct a story. It should resemble a typical newscast. In either print or broadcast journalism you would almost definitely have to start in a small market.

It's easier, though still competitive, to start as a news desk assistant or production assistant. As discussed in the chapter on television, the assistant position is where you pay your dues and learn the business. After you have proven yourself, you can pester your boss to let you do more. In a small market, that could mean writing and reporting a story. Assistants handle all of the clerical work, field incoming calls from the public, check the newswires for interesting stories, fact-check articles, possibly rewrite press releases and some headlines—basically assist with every aspect of the operation.

Career Progression

Career progression for journalists usually comes from moving to increasingly larger markets. Some journalists move several times before they're comfortable. Journalists must often be willing to pick up and move frequently and on a moment's notice if they want to advance their career. While their careers are growing, journalists continually update their résumés, clips, or videotapes and keep their eyes on other markets. Agents are always on the lookout for up-and-coming on-air talent. Frequently, if a writer or on-air personality is talented, the competing paper or station will send clips of that person's work to a bigger market in another city. Their motives are not altruistic, however. They are hoping you will be lured away, hurting their competition's ratings and improving their own. Who cares, though, if it gets you a better job. Jobs in production progress the same way. Professionals move to larger markets until they reach a level that suits their lifestyle and objectives.

Wire services offer great mobility and experience in covering all kinds of news. Stringers can get promoted to reporters in bureaus, and then transfer to bureaus in larger markets. The wire services also offer more opportunities than most news organizations for journalists interested in foreign affairs. This is because most news organizations cannot afford to maintain foreign bureaus, so they rely on wire services for their coverage of international events.

While many people dream of working in a major market like

New York, Chicago, Washington, D.C., Los Angeles, or an international bureau, most journalists do not make it to those markets, and many don't want to. They enjoy successful, rewarding careers in cities all around the country.

Salaries

Generally, entry-level salaries in print journalism are higher than in broadcasting. This is because the competition for broadcasting jobs is greater. Depending on the size of the market, $15,000 to $22,000 is an average entry-level range. However, broadcast salaries usually begin to catch and outpace print salaries after a few years. The salaries of news directors and producers in the top markets usually climb over $100,000, or can be as low as $30,000 in the smallest markets. Generally, the size of the market often indicates the size of the potential salary. Reporters in a small market, whether print, broadcast, or wire service, can earn as little as $25,000. Reporters' salaries in top markets can reach the high five and low six figures. However, burgeoning journalists should not be in it for the money. They should be focused on the fact that journalists have some of the highest career satisfaction ratings of all professions.

Strategies for Getting In

Internships, internships, internships. The Dow Jones Newspaper Fund is a nonprofit foundation sponsored by the *Wall Street Journal* that helps place students in journalism internships around the country. However, you must still be a student to get them. If you have already graduated and do not have experience, you have some catching up to do. Try to secure an internship through your college. Even if it is unpaid, it will be worth it. Volunteer on your college paper or broadcast station. It might let you obtain experience even after you have graduated. If you have moved away, the local college campus may allow you to do some volunteer work.

You can also visit the offices of any local community paper in your area. There are thousands of weekly and biweekly newspapers that not only serve as community bulletin boards but also provide local coverage that the major dailies can't. Tell them that you would like to write articles for "clips." They have nothing to lose. If for some reason they say they are not interested, write one anyway that fits their publication in tone, style, and subject matter. Drop it off in person. If they like it they will print it, and you will be on your way to your next assignment for them, or for a larger publication.

Make sure to highlight all the writing and media experience on your résumé. Obviously your cover letter must be well-written. Include samples of published writing; school newspaper writing is perfectly acceptable too.

Prepare for an interview by obtaining a copy of the periodical or viewing a station's programming to get familiar with its format and style. If applying out of town, call to obtain a copy through the mail. Viewing an out-of-town station is more difficult. If you know anyone who lives in the area, ask them to tape a few hours of the news programming for you. Send them a tape and a prepaid return envelope to make it less of an inconvenience.

Obtaining an on-air position right out of school is extremely difficult even if you do have internship experience. You're required to have a demo tape, and explaining how to make one would require another book. I suggest you take a continuing education course in broadcasting where part of the program involves making a demo tape that can be sent to stations. Learn editing skills while you are at it, because in small markets you are much more valuable if you can wear many hats. In some stations you might have to edit your own tape. In any event, it is a terrific skill to have in broadcasting, regardless of what position you are in. The basic skills are not difficult to learn. Most important: be persistent and don't take no for an answer. (See the chapter on television for insights.)

What Insiders Say

Write. Write. Write. Editors and station managers implore would-be journalists to "learn how to write the way we write." They would be happy to teach you everything else about the business, but not how to write. Practice writing for different media. Try covering your own story in ninety seconds. Listen to evening news on the television and practice writing the lead paragraph of the paper's story. You must become a news junkie and a voracious reader.

Insiders say they get frustrated when applicants send their materials in bits and pieces. Don't send the clips or tape under separate cover. Send everything in one package. It is also important to be sensitive to the news organization's schedule. You do not want to call when people are fighting a deadline.

As I mentioned earlier, most surveys show that journalists have a high degree of career satisfaction. Some journalists complain about a life of intense daily deadline pressure finally "burning them out." This deadline pressure is intensified for wire service reporters, who are under constant pressure to get breaking stories on the wires as soon as possible.

Those languishing in small markets in cities where they don't want to be are understandably frustrated. Journalists five years into their careers who have begun settling into markets and have developed extensive contacts generally enjoy a great degree of satisfaction. Journalists who have made it "big" love their jobs, citing the perks, high-profile personalities, and the ability to play to a bigger crowd.

General Information

TRADE ASSOCIATIONS
Newspaper Association of America
529 14th Street NW, Suite 440
Washington, D.C. 20045
(202) 638-4770

American Society of Journalists and Authors
1501 Broadway, Suite 1907
New York, NY 10036
(212) 997-0947

American Federation of Television and Radio Artists
(AFTRA)
260 Madison Avenue
New York, NY 10016
(212) 532-0800

The Dow Jones Newspaper Fund
P.O. Box 300
Princeton, NJ 08543–0300
(609) 452-2820

WIRE SERVICES
Associated Press
50 Rockefeller Plaza
New York, NY 10020
(212) 621-1500

United Press International
2 Penn Plaza, 18th floor
New York, NY 10001
(212) 560-1100

QUICK TIPS FOR BREAKING INTO JOURNALISM

1. Accuracy, honesty, integrity, curiosity, tenacity. Five nouns to relate to in your cover letter and interview.
2. Expand your opportunities by applying to in-house corporate newsletters.
3. Sharpen your writing and editing skills by applying to the division that is responsible for the content on a company's Web site.
4. Demonstrate your ability to produce your best work under deadline pressure through work- and school-related activities.
5. If you want to work in television or radio broadcasting, you should lose any regional accent and correct any speech problems you may have.
6. Devour information from every medium on a daily basis so that you expand your awareness of different perspectives and current events.
7. Read a high-quality newspaper every day to help sharpen your news sense and writing skills.

CHAPTER THIRTEEN

Human Resources

If you can't beat 'em—join 'em!

In many career guides, the human resources department is often called the "guardian of the gate"—the department to avoid if you want to get a job. However, human resources is not the St. Peter of the working world. While the role it plays in the hiring process is an important one, screening applicants and hiring new staff is just one of the many functions the department is responsible for.

Human resources was formerly known as the personnel department and was primarily responsible for processing and retaining employee records. However, over the past decade employers have learned that their success requires exploring new ways to tap into the resources and potential of their most important asset—their employees. Corporations are considering various methods of managing, motivating, and redefining workplace relationships.

In addition, traditional concepts of work schedules, locations, and responsibilities have been eroded by rapid technological changes that have eliminated borders and communications barriers. Simultaneously, there has been an explosion of workplace costs associated with employment litigation, health care, benefits, training, and turnover rates.

The combined effect of these revolutionary changes has redefined the role of the human resources department, which has emerged as a key management function. Human resources professionals are now strategic business partners that possess the expertise that management relies on to help manage and steer their organizations through the increasingly complex business landscape. However, business is not the only thing that is changing. As a society, family dynamics and responsibilities are changing, too. Balancing work and family pressures has become increasingly difficult and more demanding. This is especially true during an age of tumultuous mergers and downsizings, which unsettle thousands of employees in their wake.

The challenges posed by these complex professional and social issues require individuals who can think broadly and communicate effectively, individuals who can analyze problems and formulate solutions with flexibility and creativity—in other words, liberal arts graduates.

Human resources professionals apply these skills in everyday responsibilities such as sourcing and interviewing candidates, hiring new staff, establishing compensation practices, conducting training and development, creating benefits policies, mediating conflicts, and interpreting new legislation that affects people's lives and determines the way companies do business. There are approximately 400,000 individuals employed in the human resources profession, and the field is growing in size and importance.

Never before has human resources strategy played such a pivotal role in support of a company's business strategy. While many industries are in the business of investing in physical capital, the human resources profession is in the business of investing in a company's intellectual capital. That is a long-term investment guaranteed to pay dividends for many years to come.

Career Profiles

Many people narrowly view human resources simply as the department responsible for hiring and firing. Outsiders receiving a call from the human resources department are hopeful of obtaining a job, while some employees who receive a call from human resources are fearful of *losing* their job.

However, human resources has many functions that have nothing to do with entering or exiting the company, but rather fulfilling employee needs while they are *with* the company. These areas include recruitment, training and development, employee relations, and compensation and benefits. Large organizations often break down these disciplines into separate units, each headed by a human resources specialist in that area that reports to a human resources director or vice president responsible for the management and integration of all the functions. Smaller companies with fewer resources require generalists, professionals who can wear many hats and shift from role to role fluidly. Each function requires an understanding of a number of complicated issues and impacts the organization in a unique way.

Recruitment

Unlock the mysteries of the recruitment process that frustrate millions of job seekers every day. Learn how a company conducts interviews, and what questions they can and cannot ask. Recruiting requires the ability to simultaneously sell the organization and find out if the candidate is right for the job. Interviewing seems easier for the person on the hiring side of the desk than for the applicant whose stomach is doing the rumba. However, interviewing is more complicated than simply asking questions, and difficult to do effectively.

Many laws that govern all aspects of the recruiting process must be taken into consideration. They might dictate how ads and job postings are written, where they are placed, what other sources are utilized, the representation of the applicants the methods attracts, and how interviews and reference checks are conducted. The human resources department is responsible for developing employment practices and policies that comply with the laws and ensuring that the procedures are applied consistently throughout the organization. That is why human resources is often referred to as the "guardians of the gate."

Recruitment is about playing matchmaker—finding the best-qualified person that is also the best fit for the job. It is not an exact science; intuition is an important part of the process. Recruiters can distinguish themselves by demonstrating an understanding not only of the function of the department but the intangible dynamics of who is the right fit for each job.

Recruiters are often under considerable pressure because they are usually trying to fill more than one job at a time, in some cases dozens, and every hiring manager wants them filled "yesterday." The role of matchmaker can be very rewarding. It enables you to build relationships with key managers throughout the organization who rely on your resources and judgment, and with new hires who appreciate your advocacy. Watching someone you brought to the company succeed and grow within the organization is gratifying. Your efforts are having a direct positive impact on the organization and are helping to create the long-term bonds critical to the success of a human resources professional.

Training and Development

The marketplace forces that require organizations to change the way they do business also require employees to change the way they do their jobs. Organizations spend billions of dollars annually on training their employees to meet the demands of the new work environment by upgrading their technical skills.

In addition, many employees are trained to improve their oral, written, and interpersonal communication skills. Managers are trained to learn how to effectively motivate to enhance performance and resolve conflict. They are being sensitized to laws protecting and individual's rights in the workplace and are taught how to understand and manage an increasingly multicultural workforce. The training staff is also responsible for teaching standard company procedures to all employees, sometimes in conjunction with outside consultants.

Trainers must have excellent communication skills and the ability to assess the demographics of an organization to ensure that the training has a positive impact. The high-visibility training programs afford helps open many doors for career advancement.

Employee Relations

The transformation of the workplace has occurred too fast for many companies to support their employees through the transition, which negatively impacts a company's morale and ultimately leads to diminished productivity.

Employee relations can be defined as identifying and responding to the issues that affect employees personally and professionally. These individuals must develop a broad knowledge of the legislation that affect the workplace. They provide career guidance, monitor performance appraisals, resolve workplace disputes, administer disciplinary procedures, and help employees cope with personal problems. To enhance employee motivation and performance, human resources professionals who work in this area must be able to wear many hats—coach, counselor, and confidante.

Compensation and Benefits

The recruitment, training, and employee relations functions are often referred to as the "soft side" of human resources because they require more touchy-feely skills as opposed to technical skills. Also, the results of the efforts involved are not easily identifiable or quantifiable. However, compensation and benefits are hard numbers on the company's balance sheet. They represent costs that directly affect the bottom line. While both disciplines are technical and subject to a number of laws and government reporting requirements, they are of utmost importance to most employees, for they directly impact *their* bottom lines.

Health care continues to be a hot topic in the news and on Capitol Hill. The explosion of health-care costs has had a dramatic effect on families and on employers' ability to deliver quality, comprehensive coverage for their employees. Benefits personnel are responsible for designing and administering retirement, medical, disability, and related benefits packages for the firm. One of their biggest challenges is designing flexible benefit options that address the changes in work/family life dynamics sweeping our society while controlling costs.

Compensation specialists evaluate job descriptions and perform salary surveys to determine pay scales, salary increase guidelines, and bonus programs that ensure employees are paid competitively and rewarded appropriately. (Though, if their job performance was being graded by most employees, I think they would get a "D" at best!)

Entry Level

The first few months on the job should be spent absorbing the full scope of the company's operations, organizational structure, and key players. You must also master the company's policies and procedures and familiarize yourself with the company's culture. Over time, you will supplement your on-the-job apprenticeship with training seminars in each of the functional areas.

Only with this foundation can you build your career and provide the level of service required. Your first job will be that of an assistant in any of the areas. Your responsibilities will range from answering phones to sorting résumés, placing ads, processing benefits claims and salary data, coordinating training materials, and answering routine questions from employees. The key to success in an entry-level position is to demonstrate vigilant attention to detail, respect for confidentiality, discretion, maturity, and excellent interpersonal skills. You must develop a reputation that will earn you the trust and respect of employees at all levels of the organization.

Career Progression

The corporate ladder has become more like a "career web," and career progression in human resources isn't any different. Many large companies have highly compartmentalized human resources departments, with specialists in each functional area. Some of these firms allow professionals to rotate through the various disciplines before specializing in one area. Smaller human resources departments require the staff to be generalists because they must grapple with a wide range of issues every day. Your move to a management position depends on how well you understand every aspect of the profession. However, most professionals develop an affinity for one area, and you should be able to identify which area is for you within your first two years. Many liberal arts graduates are drawn to the "soft side" of the profession. However, it is a mistake to avoid considering a career in the "hard" side. As I mentioned earlier, management is ultimately responsible for ensuring that the business stays in business, so your ability to help achieve financial objectives by understanding benefits' costs and compensation practices will be beneficial to advancement of your career.

Salaries

The human resources profession offers excellent salary potential. Ranges for the various disciplines vary widely. They are dictated by the size of the company and department and the overall pay practices of the particular industry. Entry-level salaries usually average in the low to mid-twenties. Most professionals earn in the mid to high five-figure range, and management positions can easily rise well into six figures.

Strategies for Getting In

This is something that you won't hear very often in your job search: the field is not very competitive and not difficult to break into. Human resources is not yet on the radar screen as a "hot" career, partly because it is still revamping its image. Therefore, traditional job-search methods should prove fruitful. However, if you want to aid your search, you can try registering for an inexpensive human resources management continuing education course for networking contacts. Also, read the trade publications listed at the end of this section. The pages are filled with names, titles, and addresses of human resources professionals in all industries who are quoted or contribute to the publication.

The Society for Human Resources Management is the main trade association for the industry and offers various types of memberships for students and others interested in the profession. Many schools are beginning to offer human resources as a discipline on both the graduate and undergraduate levels. Check out those departments for job listings and networking contacts.

One final word of advice: Human resources is not a generic profession. It not only differs from company to company, but industry to industry. Choose an industry whose products and services interest you. Remember, the characteristics of any company or industry are usually reflected in the human resources department. If you would never want to be a lawyer, then do not work in human resources for a law firm. If, on the other hand, you find an academic environment appealing, apply to the human resources departments of colleges.

Human resources also offers opportunities for individuals interested in international issues. The human resources departments of international corporations based in the United States must also take into account the international issues that affect Americans and their families living abroad. Human resources professionals' understanding of the laws and cultures where the employees work and reside help make the transition between different locations smooth and successful.

What Insiders Say

There is usually a direct correlation between how human resources professionals feel about their jobs and the role they are asked to play by management. In most successful firms today, the human resources department has a seat in the boardroom or the ear of the CEO. Professionals in this environment typically enjoy high job satisfaction. According to one of my colleagues, "We're not just paper pushers. We are given a role in the development of management objectives and a platform for communicating those objectives to the entire organization."

However, firms entrenched in traditional, antiquated management practices generally regard the human resources department as an administrative function. "My main job is to make sure people get paid on time and that their benefits paperwork is processed," one vice president said. Individuals working in this type of environment often feel frustrated and unsupported because they are out of the loop of the business strategy.

From my own experiences, I can tell you that at its best, human resources is a dynamic profession in which you have a voice in establishing corporate objectives and the corporate culture. If you are service and people oriented, it is immensely gratifying to positively impact the professional and personal lives of your colleagues. At its worst, an understaffed and unsupported human resources department can be overwhelmingly tedious and exhaustingly reactive. Many entry-level people in human resources react most strongly to the realities of the recruitment process. "I couldn't believe how many résumés came in every day. No wonder why I didn't get many responses when I was looking for a job."

General Information

PROFESSIONAL ASSOCIATIONS
Society for Human Resources Management
1800 Duke Street
Alexandria, VA 22314
(703) 548-3440

American Society for Training and Development
1534 East 94th Street
New York, NY 11236
(212) 531-8554

American Compensation Association
14040 N. Northsight Boulevard
Scottsdale, AZ 85260
(602) 951-9191

American Benefits and Compensation Systems
380 Lexington Avenue, Suite 3610
New York, NY 10168
(212) 983-8340

TRADE PUBLICATIONS
HR Executive
747 Dresher Road, Suite 500
P.O. Box 980
Horsham, PA 19044-0980
(215) 784-0910

HR Magazine
606 N. Washington Street
Alexandria, VA 22314
(703) 548-3440

QUICK TIPS FOR BREAKING INTO HUMAN RESOURCES

1. Starting out in the recruitment function of a human resources department is one of the best ways to develop
   internal relationships, learn the company and culture of the
   various departments.
2. Consider expanding your search to include the career development office of a college. You will have direct contact
   with human resources professionals from various companies
   and industries across the country.
3. Discretion with confidential and sensitive information is
   critical in human resources. Demonstrate examples of how
   you have handled this in the past.
4. Keep in mind that health care, retail, non-profit and corporate human resources functions and environments can be
   dissimilar in many ways. Switching from one to the other
   becomes more difficult as your career advances.
5. In human resources, you must walk a fine line between
   your ultimate responsibility as a management representative, and your role as an employee advocate. Relate your
   understanding of this critical aspect of the profession to
   your own experiences.

CHAPTER FOURTEEN

Advertising

Advertising is the greatest art form of the twentieth century.

—Marshall McLuhan

Overview

Advertising is one of the most conspicuous industries in our everyday lives. Corporations spend approximately $150 billion annually to advertise their products in this country. That's greater than the gross national product of most nations! And while cave dwellers may have advertised their wares on walls and sides of stones, the omnipresence of advertising in our society is a relatively recent phenomenon. After the Second World War, the converging forces of manufacturers shifting into high gear and the emergence of television propelled advertising to the forefront of American business. Today, advertising helps the country's economy, and advertising revenues keep magazines, newspapers, and television stations afloat. Behemoths such as Proctor & Gamble and General Motors each spend over $1 billion annually on advertising. Many other Fortune 500 companies regularly spend over $100 million each year to inform consumers and persuade them to purchase their products instead of the competitor's.

Most of this money is funneled through advertising agencies, which create the messages that have become impossible for us to escape. Ads appear on billboards and buses as we walk through the streets, on pages as we flip through newspapers and magazines, on the television, on the radio, and even on the clothes we wear. Do you have a polo player or alligator on the front left pocket of your casual shirt? There are banner-toting planes at beaches and signs that catch your eye as you try to follow the action at a sports arena. It is not just the seventh-inning stretch anymore, it is the Nike seventh-inning stretch.

The advertising profession is in many ways a practical extension of your liberal arts studies. Most advertising campaigns have their roots in psychology, sociology, anthropology, and modern culture. It is a dynamic industry that requires you to keep a finger on the pulse of current trends while simultaneously staying ahead of new trends. Advertising uniquely combines quantitative analysis and artistic inspiration. The harmonic blend of these creative and quantitative skills ensures the power and the impact of a message, which must strike a responsive chord in the audience and persuade them to react in a particular way for it to be successful. That is why businesses spend staggering sums of money on advertising. The return on their investment is the conscious and subconscious influence on the decisions we make every day: what we buy, where we go, how much we spend, how we perceive products, and how we perceive ourselves.

For these reasons, advertising is frequently the subject of controversy. Some consider its pervasiveness a detrimental assault on our senses. Advertising is sometimes blamed for creating provocative messages that reinforce negative stereotypes or creating unrealistic expectations and artificial standards about what is attractive, powerful, and successful. Fashion advertising, with its waif-thin, airbrushed cover models striking unnatural poses, is frequently cited as a major offender.

Advertising is also often at the center of national moral debates. Over the last decade, Benetton has created one stir after another, with ads depicting everything from an array of colored condoms to a priest and nun locked in a decidedly unchaste embrace. However, some feel that rather than testing the limits of society's moral tolerance, advertising is merely a highly visible barometer that reflects the shifting sensibilities of the culture at large. Birth control is a hotly contested national issue, and, consequently, birth control products are conspicuous in their absence in mass-media advertising. Tobacco and alcohol are both strictly regulated products in our society, and in advertising as well. Furthermore, while some ads are criticized for their blatant sexuality, many supporters point out that sexuality in advertising is tame compared to the sexuality offered up on TV and in magazines.

Still others believe that advertising shouldn't be overanalyzed or overintellectualized. Advertising can be as benign as a Mentos commercial. Much of what the industry produces can stand on its own as pure entertainment. Many ads are designed as mini-TV shows with recurring themes, characters, and plots. Many of us have debated whether Miller Lite was better because it tasted great or was less filling, whether the Folgers Coffee couple would ever hook up, whether the pouty Calvin Klein models would ever eat, or will the Energizer Bunny ever stop going. And few among us can't sing the Oscar Mayer bologna song or haven't taken sides in the Cola wars. The Super Bowl is as much a national advertising festival as it is a major sporting event. The ads are as anticipated as the game, and frequently more memorable.

Most agree that advertising can be glamorous and high profile. It is a dynamic industry simmering with creativity, originality, and energy. While the center of the industry is in New York City, approximately 125,000 people work in more than 5,000 advertising agencies in metropolitan areas all across the country. It is a serious business that offers many exciting and fun career opportunities—especially when not taken *too* seriously. It is also fast-paced and requires lots of energy—so remember to eat your Wheaties.

Career Profiles

Advertising agencies range in size from small boutique shops of only a few people to worldwide conglomerates with thousands of employees. While the structure of an organization will vary, there are two major and distinct functions that are common across the industry: client services and creative services. The design and implementation of an advertising campaign requires teamwork, so both sides work closely together. Each offers a variety of interesting opportunities and career paths. Most people entering the industry discover early in their careers which aspect of the business interests them most and where their talents are most effectively applied.

Client Services

The individuals involved on the client services side of the business are responsible for organizing an advertising campaign for an advertiser. The most visible of the functions is the accounts department. Account executives are the liaison between the advertiser and the agency. Their role is to develop a close working relationship with the client and serve as a producer, who manages and guides all aspects of an advertising campaign.

Account executives are typically responsible for bringing new clients into the agency, sometimes aggressively wooing potential advertisers away from competing agencies, and taking care of all of the needs of existing clients. They suggest possible themes, coordinating the various agency departments to develop strategies for their clients. Account executives outline the intent, scope, and focus of the advertising strategy, communicate the client's goals to the agency, manage budgets and schedules, and work with the advertiser to achieve the most distinctive and effective campaign possible. Account executives must be excellent communicators, with strong writing and public speaking skills. In the fast-paced, often volatile world of advertising, account executives also must be quick on their feet and cool under pressure. Their efforts can mean the difference between winning and losing major accounts.

The media department plays a critical role in the design and implementation of an effective ad campaign. Researchers compile and analyze data on the various media, the demographics of the people exposed to each, how people react to different kinds of advertising in each medium, and the existing market for the product.

Media planners are responsible for analyzing the data, the client's product, and the budget. Based on research and their own judgment, media planners then develop a strategy for reaching the right audience within a given budget. For example, you are unlikely to see an advertisement for Mercedes Benz during a daytime soap opera, feminine hygiene products during World

Champion Wrestling, or Rogaine during Saturday morning cartoons on Nickelodeon. However, you will see beer commercials repeated many times during a football game, and ads for cosmetics in fashion magazines. Depending on the product and budget, where, when, how often, and in what context advertisements appear, all have a tremendous impact on the effectiveness of the advertising. A plan may suggest advertising in one medium or cross-advertising in several media with similar demographics.

Creative Services

The creative department is the force behind the advertising campaign. Copywriters and art directors work as a team to create the concept and design of an ad. All of the creative elements— words, images, and sound—come together to create an identity for a product and communicate a message to the public.

Advertising is considered a visual medium primarily because of television. But the foundation of all effective advertising is words. Copywriters must be able to generate fresh ideas and write easily under pressure. Effective advertising depends on a copywriter's skill at playing with the nuances of language to create a voice and message that speaks to the audience. Copywriters must also be in tune with various markets and trends and understand how consumers from different demographic groups think and react to various media in order to adapt the language they use accordingly. The copywriter's words, often just one line, must remind us of the company or product and evoke images of its identity (for example, GE's "We bring good things to life", or Nike's "Just do it.")

Art directors work closely with copywriters to create different concepts for an ad campaign. Art directors possess the technical skills and knowledge of design elements that help them visualize concepts and place the copywriter's words in the most effective context. Sometimes, as the cliché goes, a picture is worth a thousand words. An art director may be responsible for creating an ad in which the image itself communicates the message. When the Dairy Association wanted to remake the image of milk, for example, they launched an ad campaign featuring photographs of celebrities wearing milk mustaches. Depending on the medium, art directors may work with other artists, photographers, and producers; cast talent; select voice-over artists; and oversee the production of the finished product.

Also on the creative side are the people who work in radio and television production. A large firm will have its own in-house production department with the technical ability to produce commercials for various media. A smaller firm will have a small staff with technical ability who will work with an outside production firm to produce commercials for the agency.

Entry Level

The entry level in advertising is often an initiation. It will be a true test of your desire to make it in the industry, especially in large, competitive agencies where your first job will be as an assistant to as many as four people. When the heat is on and the environment becomes frenzied with deadline pressure, strong administrative skills, excellent organizational ability, meticulous attention to detail, a sense of humor, and a thick skin are a must. The routine clerical work may include trafficking materials to other departments, heavy telephone work, typing correspondence and memos, making lots of copies, sending faxes, picking up lunch and dry cleaning, and getting coffee.

In copywriting, you may have an opportunity to do some limited writing or proofreading. In the accounts department, you will have heavy client contact and may coordinate materials for presentations. In the media department, you may assist with research and be bogged down with tedious number-crunching. Regardless of where you start, the opportunity to learn about the business exists for those who are truly interested and have a positive attitude and the initiative to make it happen for themselves. Ask questions, pitch in, observe, and listen. Some of the larger agencies also have training programs for candidates they feel have outstanding potential. Trainees may be placed directly on an account and given exposure to the entire process of creating an ad campaign.

Career Progression

With persistence, talent, a mentor for a boss, and a little luck, you can grow to be the head of a department. Increased responsibility and promotions come from successfully taking on an increasing number of accounts and progressively larger, more complex campaigns, for more important clients. Career advancement can happen from within or by moving to another agency. Typical accounts titles include account assistant, junior or senior account executive, account executive, supervisor, and director. In media, titles progress to assistant planner or buyer, coordinator, planner or buyer, supervisor, and director. Other departments follow a similar structure of assistant titles from coordinator on up.

Meteoric rises within advertising are not uncommon—nor are plummeting fortunes. An account group can be "hot" one minute and "cold" the next as their successes or failures mount with each campaign. There is a high degree of turnover and burnout at all levels. Those who stick it out and make it in the industry thrive on the high risk/high stress/high reward environment because they find it stimulating, challenging, and fun.

Salaries

Entry-level positions usually pay around $20,000. Salaries in the $30,000 to $40,000 range in each area are not unusual after a few years. Beyond that, five to ten years out, pay can skyrocket based on how your career progresses. This is where the high reward part of the equation becomes apparent. Depending on the size of the firm, six-figure salaries at director and management levels in media, accounts, and creative services are not uncommon. However, accounts and creative services professionals are usually the highest-paid personnel in the agency.

Strategies for Getting In

The bad news is that entry-level positions turn over regularly due to the disillusionment that sets in for many entering the field. Factors like long hours, frantic pace, high competition for promotion, low pay, and mundane clerical duties are responsible for many early career casualties. There is more bad news. Those statistics do not prevent recent grads from lining up around the block as soon as positions become available. The good news, though, is that there are numerous entry-level positions available throughout the industry. Forget about the competition. As long as there are positions available, you can always figure out how to get in. The two most popular, and therefore the most competitive, areas are the accounts and creative services departments. If either of those is what you want but you aren't having any luck, set your sights on one of the less glamorous or creative areas.

The traffic department is an excellent way to break into advertising. The role of the traffic department is to keep all of the other departments operating on schedule. This group follows the ad through the departments at its various stages of completion, making sure all internal deadlines are met. They coordinate with outside vendors in the production of ad materials, all of the physical components of putting an advertisement or campaign together. Working in traffic gives you an opportunity to become familiar with all of the agency's departments and functions and to interact with the key contacts in each area. Media is another department that is usually at the bottom of the list of areas that most entry-level people try to break into. It is just as critical a component to the entire process and will provide you with exposure to other areas.

Once you are in, be open-minded and flexible. You may discover that you have a talent and interest for a particular area that you might not have considered otherwise.

Before you begin your search, you must read current and back issues of *Advertising Age,* the industry's main trade publication. The magazine covers all of the news of the industry and will help you to learn the advertising vernacular.

Since advertising is about image, your presentation is critical—both in terms of your appearance and your cover letter and résumé package. Since advertising is also about words, your cover letter will be scrutinized for writing style, clarity, and effectiveness. Agencies get stacks of letters and résumés trying to be creative and funky. That is exactly the wrong approach. The most effective advertising is remarkable in its ability to deliver a powerful message simply, such as, "Got Milk?" or "Just Do It." Understood?

What Insiders Say

"Sink or swim." "Make it happen." "Your life is not your own." "Run, run like the wind." "It is really stimulating and fun . . . never boring." Many executives revel in painting scary portraits of what it takes to succeed in advertising. They're not jaded, they've just become immune to the hordes of new graduates who descend upon the advertising community each year saying they want to be in the industry because it is "glamorous" or "cool." The entry level is often a revolving door, so it takes a lot to impress and convince them that you are going to do what it takes to pay your dues, learn the business, and stick around to enjoy all that the industry has to offer. They're the professors who scare the wits out of students the first day of class with tales of killer exams, endless reading, reams of term papers, and low grades. Many drop out and never experience the misery. They also never experience the glory.

General Information

PRIMARY TRADE ASSOCIATION

American Association of Advertising Agencies
405 Lexington Avenue
New York, NY 10174-1801
(212) 682-2500

PRIMARY TRADE PUBLICATIONS

Advertising Age
Crain Communications
220 East 42nd Street
New York, NY 10017
(212) 210-0741

Ad Week
1515 Broadway
New York, NY 10036
(212) 536-5336

Standard Directory of Advertising Agencies (Red Book)
Reed Reference Publishing
P.O. Box 31
New Providence, NJ 07974
(908) 464-6800

QUICK TIPS FOR BREAKING INTO ADVERTISING

1. Working as an assistant in the advertising sales department of a newspaper or magazine will provide you with numerous contacts from the advertising community.
2. Most large companies have internal advertising departments that produce some of their own advertising materials and campaigns, in addition to working with advertising agencies.
3. On interviews, demonstrate your understanding of the role each medium plays in communicating with consumers.
4. Advertising professionals are in the business of creating images and are acutely aware of every detail of the image you present on paper, over the telephone, and in person during interviews.
5. In your cover letter, refer to the major accounts and noteworthy ad campaigns the company you are applying to is responsible for handling.
6. Some applicants are guilty of overintellectualizing the importance of the industry in society as their reason for pursuing a career in advertising. Relax. While it is important to demonstrate a serious commitment to your job, and there are aspects of the business that serve the greater good, it is okay to also admit the undeniable universal truth for most people attracted to the industry—it is fun.

CHAPTER FIFTEEN.

Public Relations

"There is no such thing as bad publicity except your own obituary."

—Brendan Behan

Overview

Public relations is a generally misunderstood field. In fact, many people confuse it with advertising. On a basic level, public relations and advertising both involve communication and persuasion. But that is where the similarities end. Advertisements and their objectives are obvious. We know it when we see it— on television, billboards, in print—everywhere. Public relations is just as pervasive in our everyday lives, but we are often unaware of it because its methods and objectives are much more varied and subtle than those of advertising. The many different roles public relations plays, the forms it takes, and the markets it is intended for make it impossible to provide one, all-encompassing definition of public relations. It is best defined by example.

Public relations is one profession in which we all have experience. Your job search is a public relations campaign to cast you in a certain light so that someone will offer you a job. Your cover letters are actually "pitch letters," composed with the subtle nuances of language to strike just the right tone that will persuade the intended target to grant you an interview. Your résumé does not list everything you did during college (hopefully). The four years are distilled and carefully crafted into a promotional piece designed to create a specific image.

Courtships and first dates are big public relations campaigns, too. What you wear, where you go, what you say, and how you say it are all designed to influence how you are perceived. If you were nervous on the date and acted like an idiot, you may have to mount another PR campaign to reshape your image to get a second date.

In our society, the role of public relations as a formal profession has evolved and grown dramatically over the years. The field of public relations has often been equated with attention-grabbing stunts and gimmicks, and publicists have often been associated solely with celebrities, whose activities, including the scandalous ones, are planted in the gossip columns to keep them in the public's eye.

The public's awareness of the role public relations plays in the political arena has grown with the advent of television, which now plays an increasingly significant role in shaping news and in politics. The televised presidential debates in 1960 between Kennedy and Nixon broke new ground for the industry. Kennedy's image beamed through the medium as cool and confident, while Nixon, struggling under the harsh glare of the lights, sweated profusely and projected a harsh, uncomfortable persona. Viewers thought Kennedy easily won the debates. Ironically, those who listened on the radio, unaffected by the images, thought Nixon outperformed Kennedy. Now that politics had moved into the television era, the industry had new opportunities. The role of public relations in political campaign strategy was first chronicled in 1969 in *The Selling of a President,* Joe McGinnis's book that revealed how a PR campaign effectively "reshaped" Richard Nixon's image to help him win the 1968 presidential election. Since then, the partnership of politics and public relations has often been viewed suspiciously by the public.

In politics today, press secretaries act as spokespersons, providing background information to the press and promoting their politician's or political party's agenda. These individuals are nicknamed "spin doctors," because when news, scandal, or votes on legislation threaten a candidate's image, the press secretary uses the media to "spin" the news to cast their politician in the most favorable light. The public's negative perception of the link between public relations and politics is further reinforced when image-building—and frequently image-destroying—often plays a more significant role in political campaign strategies than does an in-depth analysis of the issues.

An example of how public relations shapes our lives is the Tylenol tampering scare in the 1980s. Many experts believe that Johnson & Johnson's handling of that situation was a textbook example of how the effective use of public relations in a crisis situation can protect the company's image and operations. Johnson & Johnson did not try to cover up or downplay the reports of tampering. Senior management were immediately in the public eye, communicating openly and honestly about the incidents. Johnson & Johnson reacted swiftly and empathetically to growing public concern by pulling millions of the company's product off the shelves across the country at great cost, even though authorities believed there were only three isolated incidents of poisoning. The company's actions enhanced their image and instilled the public with a sense of trust. Consumers had confidence in the company because they acted responsibly. When Johnson & Johnson said it was safe to use Tylenol again, the public believed them, a fact made evident by their reemergence as a marketplace leader.

In contrast, the Exxon *Valdez* oil tanker spill in the late 1980s illustrated how damaging a poor public relations strategy can be. When a disastrous oil spill coated hundreds of miles of the Alaskan coastline, wreaking havoc on wildlife, Exxon officials attempted to downplay the enormity of the spill, reacted slowly and inefficiently to the clean-up, and blamed the disaster on the captain of the tanker, accusing him of having been drunk. These actions, combined with images of dying, oil-slicked animals washed across the coastline, spelled a public relations disaster for Exxon. Public opinion of Exxon plummeted as massive consumer campaigns were launched to boycott the company. Thousands of Exxon gasoline credit card holders closed their accounts by mailing oil-covered cards to the company's headquarters.

Because public opinion is so powerful, individuals and organizations from every segment of society increasingly rely on the skills of public relations specialists to enhance or protect their image. Hence, the industry is growing in size and respectability. There are now more than 100,000 professionals working in the profession. Their efforts account for a significant portion of the news that reaches the public.

Whether by informing the public of a breakthrough in medical research, providing research data on various issues of public debate, or keeping us abreast of the activities of our favorite celebrities, the public relations industry offers diverse, challenging, and stimulating career opportunities for liberal arts graduates.

Career Profiles

Approximately two-thirds of the public relations professionals work in varied settings such as public and private corporations, sports and entertainment companies, governmental agencies, nonprofit foundations, and health, educational, and cultural institutions. The other third work for one of the approximately 4,000 public relations firms in the country, which range from single-person businesses to multinational organizations that employ thousands. Larger public relations firms are usually located in major metropolitan areas and often employ generalists who work in teams servicing their clients. Agencies also employ specialists, professionals from "the client side," who have firsthand knowledge of the unique dynamics of an organization or industry and know how to best conceive a plan that meets their objectives.

The structure of public relations agencies varies by size and industry. However, the range of the day-to-day responsibilities of a public relations professional are similar in any setting and often include working the phones for media contacts; writing press releases, pitch letters, and annual reports; coordinating publicity events and press conferences; and managing crises. Whether working with a broad range of clients for an agency or in-house for a specific organization, the demands of a public relations professional require the ability to adapt and react with fluidity to a variety of situations and challenges. Public relations professionals have highly developed communication skills and develop ongoing relationships with contacts from every segment of society and all aspects of the media. They have contacts with people in print, broadcast, and cable industries—basically anyone with the capacity to disseminate their message to the intended audience. In order to sustain those relationships, publicists must become trusted partners in communication, with reputations for being honest and providing accurate information.

Public relations is not about manipulation, although the practices and ethics of some are called into question. Rather, PR professionals must be intuitive—curious about what motivates human behavior and perceptions and knowledgeable about how to manage both to achieve their objectives. They must be able to grasp the heart of a problem, conceive a strategic action plan, and communicate the plan effectively to their intended audiences. Excellent public speaking and writing skills are critical. Public relations professionals must be voracious readers and information and media junkies and have their finger on the pulse of current events. The diversity of their knowledge allows them to work in many areas of an organization such as corporate communications, employee relations, community relations, product services and marketing, press relations, and public affairs. This diversity is also particularly important within a PR agency where clients may range from a sports star or celebrity trying to reshape their image, such as Courtney Love or Michael Jackson (figuratively and literally), to a nonprofit institution trying to increase corporate sponsorship and funding, such as The United Way or the (NY) Museum of Modern Art.

Finally, the diversity of the field provides you with the flexibility to work in any environment that interests you—from an agency representing clients from different industries to the PR department of a specific field—a luxury not afforded by many other occupations.

Entry Level

Most graduates are attracted to this field because of the perceived glamour. They soon realize that the profession—at the entry level and beyond—requires a lot of hard legwork, long hours, meticulous planning, and attention to detail. As in other mass-media industries, the entry level in public relations is an apprenticeship that allows you to hone your skills and adjust to the hectic pace over time. You will be on the phone constantly—answering questions, updating media contact lists, and coordinating the logistics of a media event. You will handle multiple mailings, compile mountains of research, and juggle countless other administrative duties that keep the department running. In a corporation you will likely be someone's assistant, which involves handling their clerical work as well. In a public relations firm, the entry-level title is usually account assistant. Depending on the size of the firm, you could be supporting an entire account team of as many as four people.

This will really test your organizational and interpersonal skills. However, just paying your dues by juggling administrative tasks doesn't necessarily lead to promotions. You must take the initiative by demonstrating your ability to handle increased responsibility. Participate in the process—suggest ideas, go the extra mile to accomplish tasks that you aren't expected to do. Write as often as you can and develop a reputation as a reliable, responsible contact for the various media you interact with. Talent and initiative are the two traits that lead to advancement in the profession.

Career Progression

There isn't a clearly defined career track that spans all industries. Career progression usually involves a gradual increase in responsibilities within an organization or a move to a higher-level job in another organization. Individuals five years into their career are usually in a mid-level position and enjoy the comfort of having developed enough contacts to get their message to the media without a struggle. Growth into management depends on your maturity, your understanding of the business, your ability to handle difficult situations and resolve complex problems, and the quality and breadth of your contacts.

Some agencies start entry-level employees in training programs and rotate them through different account groups. Advancement to an intermediate-level position can occur after twelve to eighteen months. Promotion to account executive, in which you are given responsibility for the day-to-day activities of one or more accounts, usually occurs within three years. Account supervisors and managers direct the programs of increasingly larger, more important accounts, and the activities of account teams. Advancement is accelerated by a record of success with difficult or complex assignments and the ability to attract new clients to the agency.

Salaries

Entry-level compensation typically ranges from $20,000 to $24,000 annually, depending on the size and location of the agency or organization. As you would expect, multimillion dollar agencies have wider pay ranges than nonprofit organizations. Department heads with more than fifteen years of experience in a large agency can earn as much as $200,000 to $300,000 per year. Salary ranges in corporations are usually slightly lower than large agencies. The lower- and middle-management levels vary greatly. Junior and senior account executives can average from the high twenties to high thirties. Supervisors and managers can double or triple that, respectively. The wide range between entry-level and management-level compensation reflects the variety of opportunity within each company and is affected primarily by your talent and initiative. The public affairs director of a nonprofit television station may earn $60,000, the director of publicity in publishing may earn $90,000, and the equivalent level within a PR agency could earn anywhere in that range or much more.

Strategies for Getting In

The same skills that bring you success in the industry also help you break into the industry. Here is where a little creativity in the job search could come in handy if traditional methods yield no returns. Think of search in terms of a PR campaign and creatively market yourself to grab an employer's attention. Write your cover letter and résumé in the form of a press release. You know I'm not one for gimmicks, but if all else fails, this approach falls within the context of the industry and therefore isn't over the top. Be persistent. Show up at the company and see if the human resources department accepts walk-in applications. Volunteer, or take a job as an intern or secretary or anything that will get you inside. Front-load your résumé with activities—school or work related—that demonstrate your ability to write and to conceive, execute, and promote an event or yourself. School newspaper, sales experience, fundraising, charity drives, student government campaigns, yard sale—are all relevant.

Become a member of the industry's primary trade association, the Public Relations Society of America, or its student chapter. It is a terrific source for networking and job opportunities. Read the PRSA newsletter and *Public Relations Journal* faithfully. These are the two primary trade publications, which are invaluable resources for networking and up-to-date industry information. Attend social and professional functions that have been coordinated by public relations professionals and strike up conversation with the representatives. This is not a profession for the shy. Sheer will and determination are often required to achieve your professional objectives. No less effort may be required to achieve your job search objectives.

What Insiders Say

One public relations veteran said he loves his job because it is fun and creative and gave me the inside scoop on the PR campaign behind one major "fun" account. He said the frenzy surrounding certain toys each year that make them "hot" and difficult to find is usually the result of a very good public relations campaign. He said it all got started with Cabbage Patch dolls, an account he had worked on. The public relations firm paid actors to wait outside a department store in a small town, then rush in when it opened to create a "frenzy" over the dolls. They did this several times in various department stores, until word got out and a local television station covered the story believing it was real. The video of "parents" climbing over each other for the limited supply of dolls was compelling enough to get picked up by the networks. These staged events created an overwhelming demand because parents didn't want their kids to be the only ones without a Cabbage Patch doll. Soon, the phenomenon swept the nation as the national news broadcast footage of real parents camping outside stores all night, then rushing in when the doors opened, hoping to grab one of the dolls. So much for ethics.

Most people in public relations do not work on such high-profile, fun accounts, however. The glamour factor is limited to the relatively small percentage of jobs in glamorous industries like sports and entertainment. But even then, many entry-level people say the glamour quickly wears off with the long hours and often tedious administrative detail work. Career satisfaction increases for those who stick it out for a few years because by then you usually have developed your own contacts and do not have to struggle to get people from the media on the phone. The keys to career advancement: contacts, excellent writing ability, and phone skills. Most professionals who advance in the field point to the diversity of responsibilities, challenges, and people they meet as the most exciting and rewarding aspects of public relations.

General Information

PRIMARY TRADE ASSOCIATION
  Public Relations Society of America
  33 Irving Place, 3rd floor
  New York, NY 10003
  (212) 995-2230

PRIMARY TRADE PUBLICATIONS
  Public Relations Journal
  33 Irving Place, 3rd floor
  New York, NY 10003
  (212) 995-2230

  O'Dwyer's Directory of Public Relations Firms
  271 Madison Avenue
  New York, NY 10016
  (212) 679-2471

QUICK TIPS FOR BREAKING INTO PUBLIC RELATIONS

1. Excellent telephone skills are critical for a career in public relations. Be prepared for a surprise telephone screening interview when you thought that a company was calling just to schedule an appointment.
2. Applicants are frequently asked to discuss how they would mount a campaign to reshape the image of a celebrity or organization. Prepare for this ahead of time.
3. Public relations writing is very specialized. Read any one of the many books available about writing for public relations. They provide numerous examples of pitch letters, press releases, and exercises to practice writing them on your own.
4. Broaden your job search to include the public relations, publicity, public affairs, and corporate communications departments of organizations in every field that interests you.
5. You must become a media and information junkie. Continually expand your knowledge of print and broadcast media outlets. Read everything, watch television, listen to the radio.

CHAPTER SIXTEEN

Before You Leap . . .

> *What is the use of running when you are on the wrong road?*
>
> —*Proverb*

What if none of the careers described in the preceding chapters interest you, and you're still not sure what you want to do? Face the disdain of your liberal arts peers by joining the ranks of the business students in consulting, pharmaceutical, sales, or Insurance? "Never!" you shout. You are a liberal arts major and there is something else, another calling . . .

Law

It is virtually impossible for any liberal arts major to go through four years of college, without, at least for a fleeting moment, flirting with the notion of becoming a lawyer. You may have been inspired by the gentle but strong, dignified character of Atticus Finch in *To Kill a Mockingbird,* moved by one of those dramatic courtroom battles in movies in which the attorney delivers a powerful closing argument, or stirred by Tom Cruise and Jack Nicholson duking it out in *A Few Good Men*. Well, do you want the truth? Are you sure you can handle the truth? Why do you think there are so many lawyer jokes? Do you know why sharks *don't* eat lawyers? Professional courtesy.

Few professionals need public relations help to improve their image more than lawyers. Even Shakespeare took his shots at lawyers. In *Henry VI,* one of the rebels against the king proclaims, "The first thing we do, let's kill all the lawyers." For the most part, though, lawyers have been portrayed glamorously by the mass media. When the television series *L.A. Law* slickly and seductively glamorized the profession in the late 1980s, law schools reported a dramatic upswing in applications and attributed it to the popularity of the show.

Obviously lawyers play an important role in our society. With each new law that affects some aspect of our personal and professional lives, lawyers are there to interpret, protect, and test the letter and limits of the law. Most of the framers of the constitution were lawyers. And considering how profoundly their work has affected us, there is much to respect of the profession. However, many believe, with good reason, that there are too many individuals practicing law and that some unnecessarily create or complicate issues for their own benefit, fueling the litigiousness of our society. Rather than enter this public debate, we will take a nonpartisan view of the facts you should consider.

There are approximately one million lawyers in the country, and the number of applications to law school do not show any signs of abating, especially as it is viewed as a lucrative profession. Your parents were right when they said, "A lawyer will never starve." Top graduates from elite law schools can command starting salaries as high as $90,000 from major law firms in big cities. Salaries can escalate to $125,000 to $300,000. If you become a partner, compensation can double or triple that. But there is a price to the high pay.

Lawyers earning those salaries typically work eighty hours per week or more, more than twice the average person's workweek. Obviously, this doesn't leave much time to enjoy all that money you are earning. And for every lawyer earning high six-figure salaries, there are many more whose compensation is in the low to high five-figure range. The average starting salaries of law school graduates hovers around $40,000. Furthermore, for every lawyer working on an exciting, high-profile case, there are thousands more handling everyday legal matters from drafting wills and finalizing real estate closings to settling misdemeanors and labor disputes. Lawyers strongly advise that anyone interested in the profession first work in a law firm or legal department of a corporation as an assistant or clerk. Individuals interested in criminal law are advised to visit a courthouse to observe that most criminal trials are a far cry from those glamorized on television.

Consult with as many lawyers from different areas of specialization as you can to learn as much as possible about the realities of the profession before you go through the rigors of law school. (Just don't forget to ask them to waive the fee.)

Teaching

No discussion about careers for liberal arts majors would be complete without mentioning teaching. Given your constant denials during the past four years, you may feel that joining the teaching ranks now would seem as if you are admitting defeat and reinforcing the stereotype—"See, you *can't* do anything else with that degree." However, teaching is not a consolation career, it is a calling. It is one of our nation's most important professions, with 3.5 million educators teaching kindergarten through the twelfth grade in school systems across the country. Most of us have been inspired by at least one teacher in our lives. And while teachers have not always been richly paid, they do rank high in the public's respect. Not only is the profession currently well-thought of in public opinion, but teachers are in strong demand, and their salaries are on the rise, too. The average public school-teacher's salary is approximately $37,000. When you consider a nine-month work year and excellent benefits, teaching no longer has to be just a labor of love. Job growth for teachers is expected to outpace most other professions in the next five to ten years. Teachers in the areas of math, science, special ed, and especially bilingual teachers are in particularly constant demand. There is more good news. The trend toward national certification is making getting your certification less of a bureaucratic nightmare. It is now easier to get certified, and for teachers to move from state to state without having to be concerned about recertification.

So, what's the catch? The working conditions of teachers still varies greatly from school to school. Many would-be teachers are dissuaded from entering the profession because new jobs are often in the poorer school districts where there is inadequate funding. Also, teachers in those school districts frequently have to compete with many socioeconomic problems their students have to deal with, making teaching even more difficult. And, with many schools in the big cities suffering from overcrowding, some teachers have resigned themselves to functioning more as school monitors than as schoolteachers.

However, teaching requires more than proficiency in a subject area. Most educators feel that the ability to overcome these challenges and make a difference in people's lives is the true art of the profession and the real reward. Teaching is physically, mentally, and emotionally challenging. And for those who have made it a career, they couldn't imagine dedicating their lives to doing anything else.

Teachers strongly suggest working as a teacher's aide or for Teach for America before committing yourself to the additional academic training and testing required for certification. There are two numbers you can call to receive information about what it takes to teach and careers in the teaching profession, or to speak with a counselor about specific questions you may have: (800) 45-TEACH and (617) 489-6407.

If you are interested in teaching at the university level, talk to as many academics as you can in the discipline you're interested in before committing to the advanced-degree studies that will be required for life in academia. Professors in the sciences, engineering, computer, and business fields usually earn much more than their humanities counterparts to keep them from entering the business world. Typical salaries for liberal arts educators range from $30,000 at the entry-level instructor position to $60,000 for full professors. The tenure track usually starts at the instructor level, from which you could become an assistant professor, associate professor, then professor. Increasingly, colleges are employing adjunct professors—part-time faculty to cut costs and lighten the load of the full-time staff. Some adjuncts are academics, while others maintain full-time careers in the business world and apply their knowledge of a special field in academia part-time. It is a convenient way to enjoy the rewards of both worlds.

Graduate School

Some liberal arts undergraduates head straight to graduate school the following fall almost out of habit. Many have difficulty conceiving of anything but school and fear the abrupt leap to the working world. Some use graduate school to delay dealing with "the whole job-search thing" because they aren't sure what they want to do. Others feel the decision to continue their education is sanctioned as smart strategy because of reports of a tight job market. However, the hallowed halls of academia should not be used as a safe haven because you are anxious about looking for a job, are having difficulty finding one, or still haven't decided what you want to do with your life. I've observed many people who have become professional students, bouncing from one degree program to another until they find themselves.

Regardless of whether or not you know what you want to do, if you plan to join the business world someday it's a good idea to spend time in the workplace gaining some perspective. Most professions do not require an advanced degree, and the few that do feel that it is beneficial for students to obtain some practical work experience before continuing their studies anyway. Much of the value of most graduate programs comes from students sharing their work and life experiences as they relate to their particular area of study. So even if you want to continue your studies simply for personal growth, graduate school is best delayed for at least a year or pursued part-time while you are working.

Before We Part

> The high prize of life, the crowning fortune of a man, is to be born with a bias to some pursuit which finds him in employment and happiness.
>
> —Ralph Waldo Emerson

Making career decisions can be daunting. But while the choices and variables are endless, never forget two things: First, you are not bound by the career decisions you make. The first job is just a first step, and if at any point you discover that you are on the wrong path, simply change your course. Second, finding a job that fires your enthusiasm is what matters most. This is not a philosophical profundity, simply a fundamental truth that most people eventually figure out.

The basic skills and strategies we have discussed will provide you with the foundation to conduct a successful job search for whatever path you decide to take. However, it is imperative that you do not confuse "basic" with "convention." The freshness of your originality should not be suppressed by the mechanics of searching for a job. Our times demand that careers be built on invention, innovation, and imagination—three traits that liberal arts majors possess in spades. You are uniquely qualified for the challenges facing employers in today's marketplace. You do not need gimmicks to compete.

I have witnessed too many candidates sabotage their job searches in incredibly creative ways over the years. Relax, it is really very simple: Be empathetic to each employer's needs and allow the fundamental methods we have discussed to unclutter your presentation so that the full dimension of your character and abilities can shine through.

And when you do find a job, also remember that careers are not about climbing ladders or racing on tracks to a finish line. Ask yourself what prize is there twenty or thirty years down the road that is so valuable that it is worth sacrificing the joy of the journey to achieve? Fulfilling and gratifying careers are achieved by creating a body of experiences that allow you to learn and grow, and on which you can reflect with pride.